THE
CATALOGUE
OF
INTERNATIONAL
CIGARETTE CARDS

COMPILED BY
THE LONDON CIGARETTE CARD COMPANY

CONTENTS

PART ONE

History and Development—*page 9*

American origins—World-wide developments—The Golden Age—The post-War period

Collecting—*page 18*

Why people collect cards—How to start collecting—Buying cards—Display and storage

How to use the catalogue—*page 23*

How to order cards—*page 24*

Index of brands—*page 25*

Books for the collector—*page 29*

PART TWO—ILLUSTRATIONS

PART THREE—THE CATALOGUE

The catalogue—*page 66*

PART ONE

HISTORY AND DEVELOPMENT

American origins

Tobacco cards originated in North America, probably during the 1870s. At that time, mechanized packaging was in its infancy and pieces of card were used inside the paper wrapping as protection for the contents. A logical development was to print colourful pictures and advertisements on the cards, but the precise date when this happened has not been established. However, a recent study of the Burdick Collection of early tobacco advertising material—housed in New York's Metropolitan Museum of Art—has revealed a card dating from around 1877.

The first cards were 'singles' unrelated in subject matter, but it was not long before enterprising manufacturers hit upon the idea of producing sequences of cards on popular themes, the object being to encourage the smoker to continue buying that particular brand in order to collect all the cards. This was the foundation of cartophily, the hobby of collecting cards, which remains popular to this day.

By the early 1880s, cigarette cards had become so well established in the USA that it was exceptional for a tobacco product not to contain one. Tobacco cards became the pop-art, culture and encyclopaedia of the masses, virtually an industry in their own right, with major firms having special departments employing well-known artists to design and produce new series. The customary format was to have a picture on one side, and an advertisement or check list of subjects on the back. Because the great majority of smokers were male, the most common themes were on actresses, beautiful women, sports, pioneering and politics, usually with an American emphasis—baseball, trotting, cowboy scenes, Indian chiefs, great Americans, State Governors, US Presidents, etc.

The phenomenal success achieved by cigarette cards in the USA led an American firm, Allen & Ginter, to introduce them to Great Britain in 1884. British companies were quick to follow the lead and by the end of the decade many were producing cards of their own.

The next major development, however, was to deal a blow to American card-lovers. In 1890, James 'Buck' Duke, head of the US company W. Duke Sons & Co (which had already swallowed up hundreds of small independent firms in the USA), masterminded the merger of five major manufacturers, Allen & Ginter, Duke, Goodwin, Kimball and Kinney, to form the giant American Tobacco Company, a move which virtually eliminated competition in the US market. The incentive for producing cards was stifled, and issues in the USA all but ceased for almost twenty years, bringing to a close the first heyday of American cards.

With the dawning of the new century, the tobacco world was shattered by a move that led to what is now referred to as the Tobacco War. William Duke, having sown up the American market, turned his attention to Britain where he bought the well-established firm of Ogdens. He then launched a massive price-cutting offensive designed to capture a large share of the British market which was second only to that of the USA. The largest British manufacturers pooled their resources and combined to form the Imperial Tobacco Company. ITC immediately counter-attacked by conducting a massive 'Buy British' campaign and a bonus scheme for retailers. They also bought an American factory to take the battle into the enemy's camp. Following a truce in 1902, the American Tobacco Company undertook to stop trading in Britain, and Imperial agreed to withdraw from the USA. It was mutually decided that the export business of both companies would be handled by an entirely new enterprise, the British American Tobacco Company.

After the formation of the British American Tobacco Company (BAT) headed by Sir William H. Wills and James B. Duke, Imperial restricted its sales to Great Britain, excluding the Channel Islands, and Ireland. The American Tobacco Company continued to operate in the USA and Cuba. Their card issues were inscribed with ATC's name, or a brand name, and usually included the factory number and district. In 1911, the US Courts ruled that ATC was a monopoly in breach of the anti-trust laws and the firm was ordered to dissolve. Duke split it into four companies, one of which retained the ATC name, famous to this day for its 'Lucky Strike' brand. The others are

Reynolds ('Camels'), Liggett & Myers ('Chesterfields') and Lorillard ('Old Gold').

Up to 1905, most early BAT issues were prepared by ATC with their net design backs and were packed with cigarettes manufactured in the USA by the old Kimball and Duke plants. As the operations of BAT spread to almost every country in the world, except for those with a government tobacco monopoly, the complexity of BAT issues developed. A quick glance at the brand index in this book will tell its own story. For the sake of simplicity, BAT issues bearing makers' names or brand names attributed to other manufacturers such as 'Havelock' and 'Capstan' (Wills) are listed in the catalogue under Wills, 'Polo' under Ogdens, 'Springbok' under UTC, etc. The BAT listing is restricted to BAT brands plus those issues with printed backs bearing no maker's name or brand, or with plain backs.

In the USA, the group of companies derived from the old American Tobacco Company continued issuing cards up to 1917. It was one of these cards which fetched the world record price of $25,000 in October, 1981. From the ATC 1912–1913 issue of *Baseball Players*, it depicts Honus Wagner of Pittsburg. Wagner forced the company to withdraw the card from circulation, hence its great rarity. However, this should not be taken as a general indication of prices, as reference to the catalogue section will show.

H.M.S. BELLEROPHON
Battleship (Sup-Dreadnought)
18,600 tons

CAPSTAN CIGARETTES

Footscray F.C.

IN EVERY BOX OF
Nº I CIGARETTES

DIXSON'S CONQUEROR
Sir Roger Champion Long Cut.

F. ABIGAIL, M.P.

World-wide developments

The early part of the twentieth century was by no means monopolized by the issues of the international giants. In almost every arena, local independent firms were in a strongly competitive environment and card issues were prolific.

In Australia, Sniders & Abraham's 'Milo', 'Peter Pan', and 'Standard' cigarettes were highly popular and this firm produced many series, often with a special local interest—*Australian Cricket Team, Australian Footballers, Australian Jockeys, Australian Racehorses, Australian Racing Scenes, Melbourne Buildings* and *Views of Victoria*. This firm's issues of cards from 1904 to 1920 spanned the Great War, hence such titles as *Australian VC's and Officers, Crests of British Warships, Great War Leaders and Warships*, and *Medals and Decorations*.

In Malta and Egypt, the firm of Cousis, among others, concentrated on photographic issues, particularly actresses, beauties and views, but also produced some unusual series: *Grand Masters of the Order of Jerusalem, Paris Exhibition* and *Popes of Rome*. Another Maltese firm, Colombos, issued several series during this period, including photographic commemorative issues on the *Life of Napoleon, Life of Nelson* and *Life of Wellington*.

In Canada, two principal companies, Tucketts and the Imperial Tobacco Company of Canada, supplied much of the home market. Four main influences can be seen in the issues of these firms. Firstly, the British heritage (Tuckett's *Boy Scout Series, British Views, British Warships*); secondly, the French connection (ITC's *L'Histoire du Canada*) reflecting the large French-speaking minority in the country; thirdly, the close ties with the USA (ITC's *Baseball Players* and *Hockey*); and fourthly, a pride in emerging nationhood (ITC's *Canadian Historical Portraits, Canadian History Series, Pictures of Canadian Life, Prominent Men of Canada*). In Imperial's case, the company's British origins are particularly marked, many of the series being reprinted from UK equivalents (*Infantry Training, Military Portraits, Modern War Weapons, Notabilities* and the *World's Dreadnoughts*).

In South Africa, there were few issues prior to 1920. The Westminster Tobacco Company, of British origin and closely linked with both Imperial and BAT, distributed *Great War Celebrities* in 1914 and their silk-fronted *Garden Flowers of the World* were issued at about the same time. United Tobacco Companies (South) Ltd produced a *1912–13 Springboks* series, *Views of South African Scenery*, and several silk issues. But it was not until the Twenties and Thirties that issues directed specifically at the South African market were produced in quantity.

As we have already seen, the 'Tobacco War' resulted in the British American Tobacco Company assuming the former overseas markets of the companies within the British-based Imperial Tobacco Company. Nevertheless, the British firms' names remained largely intact, and whilst BAT distributed the cigarettes, the brand names and indeed the names of the original firms were still used to a large extent. Thus in Australia series such as the following were issued under Wills' name in the period up to

1919: *Australian and English Cricketers, Australian and South African Cricketers, Aviation, Birds of Australasia, Melbourne Cup Winners, Prominent Australian and English Cricketers, Royal Mail, Signalling, Sporting Terms, United States Warships, Victorian Football League*, etc.

In India the 'Scissors' brand-name of Wills was dominant and among their most popular card series were various sets of *Actresses, Beauties, Boxers, Army Life, Britains Defenders, Dancing Girls, Drum Horses, Governors General of India, Heroic Deeds, Indian Regiments, Military Portraits, Regimental Pets, Types of the British Army, Victoria Cross Heroes, War Incidents*, etc. The fact that many of the purchasers would be soldiers undoubtedly had some impact on the choice of subject matter. Ogdens, with their 'Polo', 'Ruler' and 'Tabs' brands, were also noted for their card issues in India at that time, as were various BAT brands such as 'Pedro', 'Railway', 'Teal' and 'Tiger'.

BAT dominated the Far-Eastern market with their 'Pinhead' and other brands which contained cards from series such as *Chinese Modern Beauties, Chinese Heroes* and *Chinese Trades*. This company had a foothold in almost every country from Scandinavia to South Africa and Chile to China. Comparatively small local enterprises ensured that a wide choice of product was available and competition remained fierce. This was a healthy environment in which cards could play an important commercial role, and they flourished.

12

D. BRADMAN, N.S.W.

R.M.S. AQUITANIA.

ETHEL BARRYMORE

COTTON

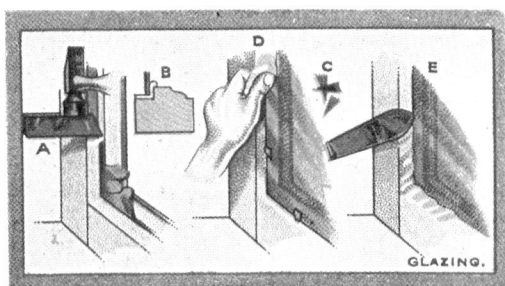
GLAZING.

LAGONDA

The Golden Age

The Great War had far-ranging effects on cigarette manufacturers. The war effort and shortages led to the suspension of card issues in the United Kingdom, and to a diminishing of issues in many other countries from 1917 to the early Twenties. But the momentum was quickly regained and led to the hey-day of card issues during the 1920s and '30s, although there were some changes. The ornate style of pre-Great War lettering and the often rather stilted descriptive texts gave way to a more functional mode. Many smaller tobacco firms either went out of business or were absorbed by larger companies. There were more women smokers and this influenced the themes chosen for cigarette cards. Most importantly, developments in entertainment, transport and a host of other innovations had a profound effect on lifestyles throughout the world and naturally enough these were reflected in card issues.

The Twenties began quietly with new issues of a generally non-military nature, which was hardly surprising after the blood-letting of the preceding years. Several popular pre-Great War British series were reprinted for issue overseas—*British Birds* and *Fish and Bait* (former Wills' series) were issued by ITC of Canada; *Riders of the World* and *Wonders of the World* (former Player's series) were issued by Wills in New Zealand; and so on. As the decade developed, the new inventions of the time began to appear on cards. Series on actresses and beauties gave way to series on film stars recording the new dominance of the cinema as the most popular medium of mass entertainment in place of the music hall. Motor cars and aviation became common subjects for cards as the automobile and aeroplane advanced from curiosities to become part of everyday life. And side by side with these issues, the ever-inventive minds of series compilers produced literally hundreds of new sets, some depicting traditional themes in a new light, others tapping entirely new pastures. Many were issued virtually world-wide, often under a variety of makers' or brand names, whilst others had only a local distribution.

In Southern Africa (and in a territory covering much of Central, East and West Africa) three principal companies, all associated with BAT, were prolific issuers of cards. African Tobacco Manufacturers (ATM) produced not only universally popular subjects such as *Animals, Cinema Stars, Popular Dogs* and the *World of Sport*, but also topics of special significance in that region: *The All Blacks' South African Tour, South African Members of the Legislative Assembly*, etc. The Westminster Tobacco Company also produced a wide range of series, those of particular local interest being *South Africa 1st* and *2nd Series*, and *South African Succulents*. However, by far the biggest firm in this part of the world was United Tobacco Companies, South, Ltd (UTC). This company produced more than a hundred different series and the texts were often in both English and Afrikaans. They were specialists in the local interest approach, the use of chauvinistic titles often revealing the independent outlook and local pride of their main market, South Africa itself: *Our Land, Our South Africa Past & Present, Our South African Birds, Our South African Flora, Our South African National Parks*, to name but a few. When war broke out in 1939, they were not slow to record South Africa's important rôle, with *South African Defence* and *Pictures of South Africa's War Effort*. Less well known in this region were Kentucky Tobacco, Kramers Tobacco and Policansky.

In North America, by this time, card issues in the USA were rare, an exception being Brown & Williamson with their aircraft series of the 1930s, but in Canada a few companies continued printing cards until the late Twenties. Tucketts, for instance, issued their series of *Aeroplanes, Aviation* and *Auction Bridge*, but BAT in one guise or another were the main producers with their 'Millbank' *Animal Cut-outs*, and ITC of Canada's twenty or so issues, many of which were reprints of British series (*Flower Culture in Pots, Gardening Hints, Merchant Ships of the World, Motor Cars, Poultry Alphabet, The Reason Why*). The British connection was not disguised; several bore the caption 'Printed in England' and one 1924 series, *Railway Engines*, was issued with Wills' name blanked out.

Australia and New Zealand at this time were a card-collector's paradise. There were the printed-back, but anonymous, issues of BAT (*Modes of Conveyance, Nature Studies*, etc). The Melbourne-based independent firm of J. J. Schuh produced some interesting series in the Twenties before becoming part of Carreras who in turn issued several series. Dudgeon & Arnell are remembered for their issue *1934 Australian Test Team*. Player's cigarettes enjoyed considerable popularity in New Zealand and this company used reprints of its own and other ITC issues for this market (*Aeroplane Series, Arms & Armour, Bonzo Dogs, Boy Scouts, British Live Stock, Dogs Heads, Lawn Tennis, Leaders of Men, Railway Working, Signalling, Whaling*, etc). But mostly this was Wills' territory, with their 'Three Castles' and 'Vice Regal' cigarettes among the top brands. A great many of the general overseas issues of this manufacturer were circulated in Australia and New Zealand. However, the distinctive flora, fauna and geography of these countries, coupled with the population's keenness for sport, made them ideal subjects for series of cards, a situation which was to be exploited by Wills' studios. *Australian Scenic Series, Australian Wild Flowers, Beautiful New Zealand, Birds of Australasia, Fish of Australasia, New Zealand Birds, New Zealand Early Scenes of Maori Life, New Zealand Footballers, New Zealand Racehorses, N.Z. Butterflies, Moths & Beetles*, and *A Sporting Holiday in New Zealand* were some of the series which resulted.

India, Malta, Gibraltar, Suez and Aden all supported substantial British garrisons throughout the 1920s and 1930s and various Wills' series were issued in these countries, usually under the 'Four Aces' or 'Scissors' label. Anonymous issues by BAT and many by Westminster were also circulated in one or more of these areas. Malta was exceptionally well served, because it benefitted also from issues by independent local firms like Atlam, Camilleri, Camler, Coussis, Mifsud & Azzopardi (*First Maltese Parliament*), Ruggier (*Story of the Knights of Malta*) and Scerri. Of these Scerri turned out a dozen or more series during this period, usually photographic in nature, some extending to more than 400 cards, and among their best known series are *Malta Views* and *Members of Parliament—Malta*.

The Far East was an immense market. Certain series by British companies were directed at the Dutch East Indies and Siam, but the vast majority concentrated on China. Wills with their 'Pirate' and 'Ruby Queen' brands circulated, among others, *Chinese Costumes, Chinese Pagodas* and *Chinese Proverbs*. In the main, though, this

Le fort Wm. Henry. Massacre perpètre par les Sauvages, en 1757.

JACK DARRAGH

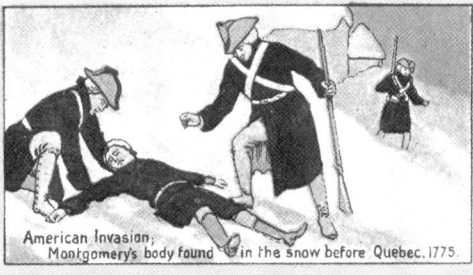

American Invasion;
Montgomery's body found in the snow before Quebec. 1775.

GEE BEE "SUPER SPORTSTER"

was British American Tobacco Company's domain, and seekers of Chinese cards will be rewarded by a glance through the BAT section of the catalogue.

One territory which has cartophilic importance far beyond its size is the Channel Islands. Some British collectors will be surprised to learn that the Channel Islands (which are British) are considered to be 'overseas' whilst Irish cards are included with 'British' issues. The explanation is historical. The Channel Islands have had for centuries a substantial degree of independence, and at the end of the Tobacco War in 1902 when the British American Tobacco Company was set up, part of the agreement was that the Imperial Tobacco Company would restrict its business to cover the United Kingdom of Great Britain and Ireland excluding the Channel Islands. Hence the Channel Islands' unique place in cartophily. The Churchman's, Player's and Wills' sections of this catalogue begin with a list of Channel Islands issues, all dating from the Twenties and Thirties, and all similar to mainland issues except for the exclusion of album clauses and the like from their texts. BAT circulated a number of their own issues such as the 1931 series of *Pre-historic Animals* and *Safety First* in this territory, as well as producing *Channel Islands Past & Present* exclusively for this market. Bucktrout, BAT's associate company in Guernsey were responsible for several issues including a local interest series *Football Teams of the Bailiwick*. The Guernsey Tobacco Company (also BAT) issued under its own name some of Wills' *A Famous Picture Series*. The Jersey Tobacco Co produced a series of *Miniature Playing Cards* in 1933, and Simonets gave birth to several issues. In earlier times, the Cigarette Company, Jersey, produced its *Jersey Footballers*.

The European mainland had been slow to follow the example set by Britain in issuing cigarette cards. This was primarily due to the fact that the Governments of most of these countries operated a State tobacco monopoly in which competition, and therefore cigarette cards, had no part to play. Nonetheless, the situation altered to some degree in the Twenties and Thirties. In Denmark, J. & R. Bell produced two series. In Belgium and the Belgian Congo BAT issued a number of French language series in their 'Albert' brand. In Switzerland, the same firm's local subsidiary issued their series *Actrices*, and Melachrino & Co produced three series of *Peuple Exotiques*.

With one or two exceptions, production of cigarette cards was halted in 1940, bringing to a close the golden age of cigarette cards.

ANTILOPE BONGO

WEST PARK PAVILION, JERSEY

BELLES VUES
de BELGIQUE

N° 45

ANVERS
FONTAINE DU BRABO
La Grand'Place d'Anvers est déco-
rée de la curieuse fontaine du Brabo,
représentant ce héros légendaire, au
moment où il jette dans l'Escaut la
main du géant Antigonus. Ce géant
prélevait un impôt sur tous ceux qui
parcouraient le fleuve, et il coupait
la main à tous ceux qui refusaient ce
tribut. De cette légende vient le nom
d'Anvers (hand, main, werpen, jeter.)

Cigarettes
Albert

S.S. "ISLE OF JERSEY"

PINE SISKIN
Spinus pinus

NO. 34

The post-War period

To the great disappointment of many thousands of card collectors all over the world, the end of hostilities did not herald the resumption of cigarette card issues. It is true that in 1947, Benson & Hedges of Canada came out with their series of *Ancient & Modern Fire-Fighting Equipment*. In the early Sixties, there was a minor flurry of activity when BAT (in their 'Domino' brand) produced French language issues for the Mauritius market (amongst these are some of the cheapest cards in the catalogue); and the Jersey company Ching & Co are to be applauded for distributing several of their own series (these, too, being still very reasonably priced). The General Cigar Company of Canada also deserves a mention for its 1968 issue of *Northern Birds*.

Whether or not tobacco cards will ever return on any substantial scale is anybody's guess. But there are two hopeful signs: firstly, the issue of 'trade' cards, that is those picture cards issued with non-tobacco products, continues unabated in many countries. Secondly, two major manufacturers, Player's and Wills, have both begun issuing cards with their small cigars sold in Britain. Evidently this has proved successful because the number of brands containing these cards has been increased. Cartophilists will certainly hope that this may mark the beginning of a second golden age when cigarette cards will once more be packed in hundreds of different brands, right around the globe.

COLLECTING

Why people collect cards

The world contains only two types of people: those who collect and those who do not. The first issuers of cards were quick to recognize that the collecting instinct was strong, regardless of race or creed, irrespective of culture or position in life, and unrestricted by geographical boundaries. In consequence, cigarette cards became a world-wide phenomenon, and the hobby of collecting them has been enjoyed for generations by countless millions of ordinary men and women, and remains popular to this day. As with most fields of activity, individuals have their own preferences, and this is reflected in what they collect.

Firstly, there are the thematic collectors, those who are interested in a particular subject and wish to obtain the pictures and information relating to it. Almost every subject imaginable has a following, and such is the vast range of series available that few interests are not covered. Amongst the most popular are railways, motor cars, military matters, the cinema and various sports. Not surprisingly, each of these topics has appeared in numerous series, in some cases so much so that the collector is often able to specialize in just one aspect, for example, cinema stars of the 1930s.

Other collectors concentrate on the issues produced in their own country or those relating to it. In this context it is worth mentioning here that certain British issues for the home market (of which information can be found in *The Complete Catalogue of British Cigarette Cards*) have a direct relevance in other countries; for example, Wills' *Overseas Dominions (Australia)*, Hills' *Views of Interest (Canada)*, CWS's *African Types*, etc.

Another area of specialization is to collect the issues of a particular manufacturer regardless of subject matter or country of origin; or to take a method of printing such as early colour lithography, photogravure, real photographs, etc. Here, for students of the art of printing, there is a comprehensive visual record of printing developments during the past hundred years. And it is not only the changes in printing techniques that can be traced, but also fashions in type-faces and styles of graphic ornamentation.

Because cards faithfully reflect the age in which they were issued, there are collectors who enjoy cards from just one decade, a monarch's reign, or some other clearly defined period. A broadly-based collection built up in this way will show the royal, political, military, sporting and entertainment personalities of that time, the modes of transport, great events, the achievements and discoveries of the generation, and its hopes, aspirations and fears. Nostalgia has a part to play: memories of happy days can be swiftly rekindled as the collector immerses himself in cards from an earlier period in his or her own life.

Cigarette cards are a very accurate source of reference material, and both the texts and illustrations are frequently consulted by historians, researchers and authors. A set of cigarette cards will more often than not use its pictures to tell a story or to impart knowledge. Do you know of a set of stamps which runs to fifty closely related illustrations accompanied by enough factual information to write a book? That is why cigarette cards have a fascination that is all their own.

In another category are 'type' collectors, those who collect a single card (or two cards to display side by side to show a typical front and back) from a series, rather than a complete set. This may be because sets are simply not available, as is sometimes the case with particularly rare and expensive cards, but often it is a convenient method by which a person of limited means with an ambitious collecting aim can obtain a representative selection of the cards he requires. Many collectors compromise by having complete sets of the more reasonably priced series, accompanied by selected examples of the rarer issues. This is not to imply that card collectors need large bank accounts. A search through the catalogue section of this book will reveal some complete sets of cards in prime condition on sale at less than one pound sterling. And bearing in mind that sets most commonly comprise twenty-five or fifty cards, compare those prices with what you would have to pay for stamps and other collectors' items of equal age and condition.

How to start collecting

For newcomers to the hobby, the sheer variety to choose from may at first seem a little daunting. A good starting point would be to scan the catalogue at the back of this book and make a list of the series which seem 'probables' for both content and price. Many are illustrated in the central section of this book but otherwise you might decide to purchase an odd card from each of the series concerned to make sure they come up to expectations before buying the complete set. If the amount of money available is somewhat limited, it may be worth considering whether to start with modern trade issues, most of which cost less than one pound sterling per set. Various reference works, catalogues and a magazine will also prove to be of considerable help, and these are listed on page 29. Amongst them, *The Catalogue of British Cigarette Cards 1888 to 1983*, with listings of thousands of different series, many of which are illustrated in full colour, will give an even broader base to your collecting. The *Trade Card Catalogue* lists around 4000 series of cards issued with products other than tobacco during the past hundred years.

Cigarette Card News and Trade Card Chronicle is a magazine which has been published regularly since 1933. Posted monthly to subscribers in more than thirty countries, it contains articles by expert contributors including detailed information about new series of cards as they are produced, advertisements and announcements of interest to collectors, special lists with money-saving offers, free catalogues for public and postal auctions, and free sample cards from certain new issues.

Buying cards

Many readers will already have collections of cards which they wish to augment or improve. Other readers will be complete novices. For both groups, the advice is the same: make sure you get value for money. One factor is of over-riding importance and that is the condition of the cards. As with all collectors' items, damaged goods are a lot less valuable than those in top condition. The prices quoted in the catalogue section are selling prices for top quality cards from the London Cigarette Card Company Limited, a large and reputable business which has been dealing with collectors all over the world since 1927. On page 24 you will find information on how to obtain the cards you want.

You may also wish to buy cards in auction, and here again the London Cigarette Card Company can help. Six times a year, the company holds major auctions at Caxton Hall in London. The auction catalogues are sent out a month or six weeks in advance, free to subscribers of *Cigarette Card News*, or on application. The auction department takes great pains to describe each lot accurately, including the all-important condition of the cards. You do not have to be present in the room in order to take part because collectors from both Britain and abroad can bid by post, confident that they will receive goods which match the description. This is not true of all auctions, especially those run by non-specialists who include a few cigarette cards as part of a general sale, not because they intend to deceive but because they do not have the expertise to evaluate condition.

For most collectors, the investment potential of cards is of secondary importance; pleasure is derived from the cards themselves. Nonetheless, prices have increased over the years, partly because of inflation but also because collecting is now more popular than at any time since the War. Unlike many commodities which can be manufactured to meet demand, supplies of cigarette cards are limited to those already in circulation. The growth in card values has been steady rather than spectacular. There are not the frantic leaps and plunges associated with the gold market or the stock exchange. Most collectors will scorn financial profit as a motivation, but few will not gain a certain satisfaction from the knowledge that their cards are now more valuable than when they were bought. It is undoubtedly true that wise buying has in the past proved to be a sound long-term investment. But anybody who imagines he will be able to buy cards to resell at a profit in a few months time will be disappointed.

The majority of collectors will keep their cards for many years and will obtain lasting enjoyment from them. However, because of their comparatively fragile nature, cards are easily damaged, and careless handling can greatly reduce a collection's value. How you store your cards is vitally important.

Display and storage

If cards are not stored under the correct conditions, all sorts of heart-breaking mishaps can occur. Strong sunlight can lead to fading, dust will make the outer surfaces dirty, bookworms or other undesirables will wreak havoc. Never use rubber bands because over a long period indentations will appear wherever contact is made; also the rubber may destabilize and stain your cards. The worst enemy is moisture which can lead to mildew, buckling and sticking together. Ideally, cards should be stored in a dry room with an even temperature, and, of course, out of the reach of young children or pets.

If you intend neither to look at your cards nor to handle them, they may be wrapped in paper for storage in drawers until required. Special transparent wrapping strips are available in various sizes. But most collectors will want to view their cards, and there is a range of albums designed especially for this purpose. These are loose-leaf binders housing plastic leaves with pockets into which the cards can be slipped. Once in place, the full area of both the front and the back of each card is displayed. Access is simplicity itself, and the plastic film protects the cards from the effects of handling. Different sizes of card can be accommodated in the same album, and pages can be added or removed at will for easy re-arrangement. Spaces at the margins of the leaves and a pocket on the album's outer spine are useful for inserting notes and index references. Full details of these albums will be found in the advertisement on page 21.

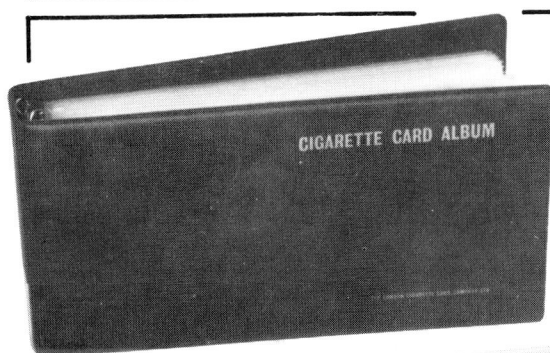

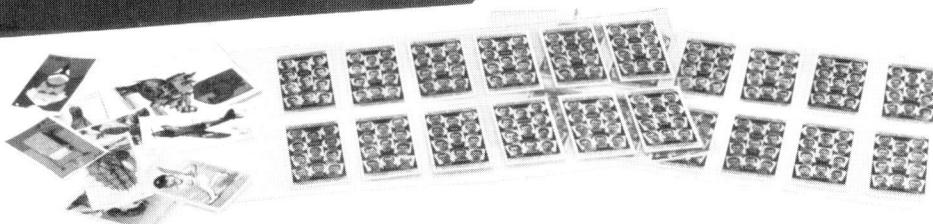

HOW TO USE THE CATALOGUE

This catalogue excludes cigarette cards issued for the British home market. It does not purport to be complete in the sense of containing every single series ever produced, because that would be an impossible task. But it does include most of the cards that collectors are likely to come across in pursuit of their hobby.

Manufacturers are listed in alphabetical order, and the issues of each firm are catalogued alphabetically within suitable sub-divisions such as 'with brand name', 'without brand name', 'silks' etc. Where a brand name, but no maker's name, is shown on the card, reference should be made to the Index of Brands. Cards with printed backs but no brand or maker's name, and cards with plain backs, are listed under the firms to which the issue has been attributed.

Information is given in the columns from left to right as follows:

Illustration Number: The number corresponds to the numbered illustration in the central section of the book.

Size and Printing: The absence of a code letter indicates that the series is of standard size (approximately 68×36 mm). A code letter 'L' defines the card as being large (about 80×62 mm). Other codes are 'K' = smaller than standard, 'M' = between standard and large, and 'EL' = larger than large. The letter 'P' is used to show that a series consists of photographs.

Number in Set: This figure gives the number of cards in the series. A question mark alongside shows that the exact number is unknown.

Title and Date: Where a series title is printed on the cards, this is used in the catalogue. For cards which do not exhibit a series title, an 'adopted' title is shown. In cases where a firm issued several different series with the same title, these are distinguished by the addition of code letters 'A', 'B', and so on; these may be further subdivided into 'Set 1', 'Set 2', etc. The date is shown where known.

Reference Code: 'RB18' followed by a number refers to the *B.A.T. and Tobacco War* reference book. 'WI' and 'WII' refer to the *World Tobacco Index Part I* and *Part II* respectively. A reference number following a Wills' series relates to the *Wills' Reference Book*. (Details of these publications will be found on page 29).

Prices: The last two columns show the London Cigarette Card Company's selling price for odd cards and complete sets in very good condition. Where no price is shown, this does not necessarily mean that the Company are permanently unable to supply, and if you require items in this category, please request a quotation enclosing a self-addressed envelope either with an International Reply Coupon or ready-stamped for posting in Britain.

HOW TO ORDER CARDS

Availability

We have enormous stocks of cigarette cards and the chances are that we will be able to supply your requirements for most series. However, certain cards, particularly from rarer series, may not be available in top condition and in such cases it is helpful if you state whether cards of a lower standard are acceptable at a reduced price. If a complete set is not in stock, we may be able to offer a part set with one or two cards missing, at the appropriate percentage of full catalogue price. In some instances we can supply sets on request in fair to good condition at half catalogue price. If you are in doubt as to availability, we will be happy to quote on receipt of a self-addressed envelope, either ready-stamped for posting in the UK or accompanied by an International Reply Coupon.

End Numbers

When ordering odd cards, please allow treble price for end numbers, for example numbers 1 and 50 of a set of fifty. These are the cards most frequently damaged in collections and are more difficult to obtain in top condition.

Post, Packing and V.A.T.

An extra charge for postage and packing is made on all orders for cards, based on current UK postal rates and depending on the weight of the package. Please allow for this in your remittance. Any difference will be invoiced as a debit or credit to be carried forward to your next order. At the time when this catalogue was published, cards were zero-rated for Value Added Tax (VAT) but postage and packing is classed as a service and is subject to VAT at the prevailing rate. Orders for delivery outside the United Kingdom are free of VAT (this includes the Channel Islands, Eire and British Forces Post Offices abroad).

Ordering

Please ensure that your name and full address are shown clearly. State the maker's name and set title required (with 'first series', 'set 1', date of issue, etc., where the distinction is necessary). For odd cards, please list each individual number wanted. If the order is to be sent to an address outside Europe, please specify whether it should be posted by surface or airmail. Make your cheque payable to the London Cigarette Card Company Limited and enclose with order. Banknotes should be sent by registered post. Cheques and banknotes in the local currencies of most countries are acceptable and will be credited after conversion at the daily rate, less bank charges. Send your order to:

> The London Cigarette Card Company Limited,
> Sutton Road,
> Somerton,
> Somerset. TA11 6QP
> England.

Guarantee

In the unlikely event that you, the collector, are not satisfied with the cards supplied, we guarantee to replace them or refund your money provided you return the goods immediately. This guarantee does not affect your statutory rights.

INDEX OF BRANDS

Admiral Cigarettes—see National
    Cigarette & Tobacco Co.
Albert Cigarettes—see British American
    Tobacco Co.
S. Anargyros—see American Tobacco
    Co.

Between the Acts—see American
    Tobacco Co.
Big Run Cigarettes—see American
    Tobacco Co.
Black Spot Cigarettes—see Scerri
British Consuls—see Macdonald
Broadleaf Cigarettes—see American
    Tobacco Co.

Cairo Monopol Cigarettes—see
    American Tobacco Co.
Carolina Brights—see American
    Tobacco Co.
Copain Cigarettes—see British American
    Tobacco Co.
Coronet Cigarettes—see Sniders &
    Abrahams
Cycle Cigarettes—see American
    Tobacco Co.

Derby Little Cigars—see American
    Tobacco Co.
Domino Cigarettes—see British
    American Tobacco Co.

Egyptienne Luxury—see American
    Tobacco Co.
Emblem Cigarettes—see American
    Tobacco Co.

Fez Cigarettes—see American Tobacco
    Co.
Fume Emblem—see Westminster
    Tobacco Co.

Gold Coin Tobacco—see Buchner

Hassan Cigarettes—see American
    Tobacco Co.
Havelock Cigarettes—see Wills
Helmar Cigarettes—see American
    Tobacco Co.
Herbert Tareyton Cigarettes—see
    American Tobacco Co.
Hindu Cigarettes—see American
    Tobacco Co.
Hoffman House Magnums—see
    American Tobacco Co.

Honest Long Cut—see Duke or
American Tobacco Co.
Hustler Little Cigars—see American
Tobacco Co.

Islander, Fags, Specials, Cubs—see
Bucktrout

Jack Rose Little Cigars—see American
Tobacco Co.
Just Suits Cut Plug—see American
Tobacco Co.

Kopec Cigarettes—see American
Tobacco Co.

Lennox Cigarettes—see American
Tobacco Co.
Le Roy Cigars—see Miller
Lifeboat Cigarettes—see United
Tobacco Co.
Lotus Cigarettes—see United Tobacco
Co.
Lucky Strike Cigarettes—see American
Tobacco Co.
Luxury Cigarettes—see American
Tobacco Co.

Magpie Cigarettes—see Schuh
Mascot Cigarettes—see British American
Tobacco Co.
Mecca Cigarettes—see American
Tobacco Co.
Milo Cigarettes—see Sniders &
Abrahams
Miners Extra Smoking Tobacco—see
American Tobacco Co.
Mogul Cigarettes—see American
Tobacco Co.
Murad Cigarettes—see American
Tobacco Co.

Nebo Cigarettes—see American
Tobacco Co.

OK Cigarettes—see African Tobacco
Mfrs.
Obak Cigarettes—see American
Tobacco Co.
Officers Mess Cigarettes—see African
Tobacco Mfrs.
Old Gold Cigarettes—see American
Tobacco Co.
Old Judge Cigarettes—see Goodwin
Old Mills Cigarettes—see American
Tobacco Co.
One of the Finest—see Buchner
Our Little Beauties—see Allen &
Ginter
Oxford Cigarettes—see American
Tobacco Co.

Pan Handle—see American Tobacco Co.

Perfection Cigarettes—see American Tobacco Co.

Peter Pan Cigarettes—see Sniders & Abrahams

Picadilly Little Cigars—see American Tobacco Co.

Piedmont Cigarettes—see American Tobacco Co.

Pinhead Cigarettes—see British American Tobacco Co.

Pirate Cigarettes—see Wills

Polo Bear Cigarettes—see American Tobacco Co.

Puritan Little Cigars—see American Tobacco Co.

Purple Mountain Cigarettes—see Wills

Recruit Little Cigars—see American Tobacco Co.

Red Cross—see Lorillard or American Tobacco Co.

Richmond Gem Cigarettes—see Allen & Ginter

Richmond Straight Cut Cigarettes—see American Tobacco Co.

Royal Bengal Little Cigars—see American Tobacco Co.

St. Leger Little Cigars—see American Tobacco Co.

Scots Cigarettes—see African Tobacco Mfrs.

Scrap Iron Scrap—see American Tobacco Co.

Senator Cigarettes—see Scerri

Sensation Cut Plug—see Lorillard

Silko Cigarettes—see American Tobacco Co.

Sovereign Cigarettes—see American Tobacco Co.

Springbok Cigarettes—see United Tobacco Co.

Standard Cigarettes—see Carreras or Sniders & Abrahams

Sub Rosa Cigarros—see American Tobacco Co.

Sultan Cigarettes—see American Tobacco Co.

Sweet Caporal—see Kinney or American Tobacco Co. or ITC Canada

Sweet Lavender—see Kimball

Teal Cigarettes—see British American Tobacco Co.

Three Bells Cigarettes—see Bell

Tiger Cigarettes—see British American Tobacco Co.

Tokio Cigarettes—see American Tobacco Co.

Tolstoy Cigarettes—see American
   Tobacco Co.
Trumps Long Cut—see Moore & Calvi
Turf Cigarettes—see Carreras
Turkey Red Cigarettes—see American
   Tobacco Co.
Turkish Trophy Cigarettes—see
   American Tobacco Co.
Twelfth Night Cigarettes—see American
   Tobacco Co.

U.S. Marine—see American Tobacco
   Co.
Uzit Cigarettes—see American Tobacco
   Co.

Vanity Fair Cigarettes—see Kimball
Vice Regal Cigarettes—see Wills

Virginia Brights Cigarettes—see Allen &
   Ginter
Wings Cigarettes—see Brown &
   Williamson

BOOKS FOR THE COLLECTOR

Catalogues and Handbooks

The Catalogue of British Cigarette Cards, 1983 Edition
Catalogue of British cigarette card issues from 1888 to 1983. Gives
selling prices for odd cards and sets in first class condition from our
extensive stocks. Details of over 4,000 series .... £5.00 post free

The Complete Illustrated Catalogue of British Cigarette Cards, 1983 Edition
A highly readable history of cigarette cards from their origins to
the present day, with special chapters on collecting. Full size
coloured illustrations of cards from more than 600 series plus a
special pictorial feature on railways. The book includes the
Catalogue of British Cigarette Cards from 1888 to 1983 (as detailed
above).. £12.95
plus £1.80 post

The International Catalogue of Cigarette Cards
With over 200 colour illustrations, this companion volume to the
above book, contains sections on the history and development of
international cards. Details of over 2000 series.................. £7.95
plus £1.20 post

Trade Card Catalogue (1983 edition). Gives selling prices for odd
cards and sets in first-class condition from our extensive stocks.
Details of over 4000 series .... £3.50 post free

Handbook Part I ('H' reference). British cigarette card issues 1888
to 1919. 172 pages of listings of un-numbered series, illustrations,
etc... £4.50 post free

Handbook Part II ('Ha' reference). British cigarette card issues
1920 to 1940, plus amendments and additions to Part I. 164 pages
of listings of un-numbered series, illustrations, etc............ £4.50 post free

Other reference books

Collecting Cigarette Cards and other Trade Issues by Dorothy
Bagnall. An illustrated paperback .... £3.50 post free
Directory of British Issuers................................. £1.50 post free
Glossary of Cartophilic Terms............................... £1.50 post free
Issues of Abdulla/Adkin/Anstie.............................. £1.50 post free
Issues of Ardath.. £1.50 post free
Issues of Churchman... £1.50 post free
Issues of Faulkner.. £1.50 post free
Issues of Gallaher.. £1.50 post free
Issues of Hill.. £1.50 post free
Issues of Lambert & Butler.................................. £1.50 post free
Issues of Godfrey Phillips.................................. £1.50 post free
Issues of Player.. £1.50 post free
Issues of Taddy... £1.50 post free
Wills Reference Book.. £5.00 post free
Ogdens and Guinea Gold Reference Book .... £10.00 post free
B.A.T. and Tobacco War Reference Book....................... £10.00 post free
British Trade Index Part I (pre-1945 issues)................ £7.00 post free
World Tobacco Index Part I .... £10.00 post free
World Tobacco Index Part II .... £10.00 post free
World Tobacco Index Part III................................ £10.00 post free
Guide Book No 1 — Ty-Phoo Tea Cards......................... £1.50 post free
Guide Book No 2 — F. & J. Smith Cards....................... £2.00 post free
Guide Book No 3 — A. & B. C. Gum Cards...................... £2.75 post free

All the above books are available from
**THE LONDON CIGARETTE CARD COMPANY LTD.,
SUTTON ROAD, SOMERTON, SOMERSET, TA11 6QP**
Tel. Somerton (0458) 73452

PART TWO

Put up or Shut up.

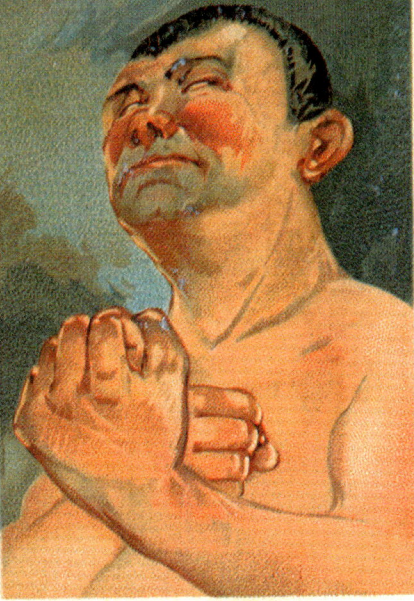

W. Duke Sons & Co. N.Y.
HONEST LONG CUT
SMOKING AND
CHEWING TOBACCO.

Sea Bream.

S. S. TEKAPO.

Death of Brock at Queenstown Heights, 1812.

S.S. EMPRESS OF AUSTRALIA.

COURSING

LESSER YELLOWLEGS
Totanus flavipes

NO. 14

LORD HOTHAM'S ACTION, 1795

No. 12

Cambos'
Aristocratic Cigarettes

ARTHUR G. HAVERS

The Niblick in a Bunker.
Finish of the Swing.

EGYPTIAN HARP

W. Duke Sons & Co.
The Largest Cigarette
Manufacturers in the World.

Card 1

Card 3

U.S.S.CO'S.

STEAMERS
A SERIES OF 50.

40

S.S. TEKAPO.
WELLINGTON

Length, 291ft.; breadth, 38.6
ft.; 2,350 tons (gross); 1,500 h.p.;
10 knots. Built in 1881 by R.
Steel & Co., Greenock. Passengers, 120 first, 60 second. She
was originally named Cape Clear.
Purchased in 1884. She was the
U.S.S. Co.'s first vessel in the
Calcutta trade. She was wrecked
near Sydney Heads in 1899.

DOMINION TOBACCO CO.LTD.

Card 4

CANADIAN HISTORY
SERIES OF 48

40.
Death of Brock at Queenstown
Heights, 1812.

General Isaac Brock
was commander in Upper
Canada when hostilities
broke out between Ameri-
ca and Britain in 1812. He
successfully repelled the
American attack and dur-
ing the offensive defeated
General Hull who surren-
dered with 2500 men and
33 cannon. Meanwhile
General Van Rensselaer
was leading another force
which gained a position at
Queenstown Heights. Af-
ter a desperate fight the
Americans were again de-
feated, but at terrible cost.
Canada lost her hero, who
fell while leading his troops.

IMPERIAL TOBACCO COMPANY
OF CANADA LIMITED

No 1236i

Card 5

MERCHANT SHIPS
OF THE WORLD
A SERIES OF 50.

5

The S.S. "Empress of Aus-
tralia," 21,850 tons, 615 feet in
length, burning oil fuel, and
carrying 400 first, 165 second,
1,000 third class passengers, is
on the Canadian Pacific service
to Japan and China. A very
interesting feature of her first
class passenger accommodation
is that all the cabins are fitted
with bedsteads, there being no
upper berths. The public rooms
are most beautifully decorated
in Louis XVI. style. There is
also a swimming bath decorated
in Pompeian style.

ISSUED BY
IMPERIAL TOBACCO COMPANY
OF CANADA, LIMITED.

BOBl.   PRINTED IN ENGLAND.

Card 7

GAMES AND SPORTS SERIES
Published by
OLD JUDGE CIGARETTE FACTORY
GOODWIN & Co.,
NEW YORK.

JULIUS BIEN & CO. LITH. N.Y.

ARCHERY
ANCIENT TOURNAMENT
BASE BALL FIELDER
" CATCHER
" PITCHER
" BATTER
BULL FIGHT
BILLIARDS
BICYCLING
BOWLING
BOXING
CANDLING
CHARIOT RACE
CURLING
CLUB SWINGING
COURSING
CRICKET
DUMB-BELL RAISING
FISHING
FOOT BALL
FOOT RACE
FOX HUNT
FENCING
GLADIATORS
HARE AND HOUNDS
HURDLE RACE
HAND BALL
HIGH JUMPING
ICE YACHTING
LAWN TENNIS
LACROSSE
POLE VAULTING
PUTTING THE SHOT
PISTOL SHOOTING
PEDESTRIAN CONTEST
POLO
PIGEON SHOOTING
QUOITS
ROLLER SKATING
RUNNING RACE
SKATING
SNOW SHOEING
SKITTLES
SWIMMING
SHUTTLE COCK
TOBOGGANING
THROWING THE HAMMER
YACHTING

Card 8

Musical Instruments
PACKED IN
DUKE'S CIGARETTES.

ACCORDEON   HUNTING HORN
BAGPIPE   HURDY GURDY
BANJO   JEWS HARP
BASS DRUM   KETTLE DRUM
BASS VIOL   LUTE
BASSOON   LYRE
BELLS   MANDOLIN
BONES   OBOE
BUGLE   ORGAN
CASTANETS   PANDEAN PIPES
CLARINET   PIANO
COACHING HORN   ROMAN HORN
CONCERTINA   S XOPHONE
CORNET   SEl EIM
CYMBALS   SPINET
DRUM   TAM TAM
EGYPTIAN HARP   TAMBOURINE
FIFE   TRIANGLE
FLUTE   TROMBONE
FRENCH HORN   TUBA
GUITAR   TUMBLERS
HAND ORGAN   VIOLIN
HARMONICA   VIOLINCELLO
HARP   XYLOPHONE
HERALDS TRUMPET   ZITHER

MANUFACTURED BY
W. DUKE SONS & CO.
NEW YORK & DURHAM, N.C.

SCHUMACHER & ETTLINGER N.Y.

Card 9

HOW TO PLAY
GOLF
A SERIES OF 50

No. 19

The Niblick in a Bunker.

Finish of the Swing.

The turf or sand should be
taken immediately behind
the ball, driving the club
head through the turf or
sand with the right hand
and wrist. Finish with the
arms well out. Keep your
feet.

*Be sure you do not ground your
club in a bunker.*

ISSUED BY
IMPERIAL TOBACCO COMPANY
OF CANADA, LIMITED

10763   PRINTED IN ENGLAND

Card 2

HONEST LONG CUT
SMOKING & CHEWING TOBACCO

Boss of the ward.
But you ought to see the other feller!
Cullie.
Drunk again and glad of it.
Get on to his Nobs.
Gussie.
He's bin there before.
In The Soup.
Jay.
Jim Dandy.
Jolly Cop.
Lah ! ah.
No flies on him.
Off his Base.
Oh, what a night!
Old Hoss.
On the Dead Quiet.
On the Q. T.
On the Rialto.
Put up or shut up.
Rats.
Ripper.
True Stripe.
What er i given us?
You know!

W. DUKE SONS & Co.,
NEW YORK.

GEO. S. HARRIS & SONS. LITH. PHILA.

Card 6

NORTHERN BIRDS BY FENWICK LANSDOWNE

One of our commonest shore birds, this
gray and white sandpiper is seen in large
numbers on prairie ponds during spring
and fall migrations. It nests from Alaska
and the Yukon southward, and winters
from the Gulf of Mexico all the way to
Argentina.

Très commun sur nos rivages, on peut
voir ce chevalier gris et blanc en groupes
nombreux près des marais des prairies
durant les époques de migration du prin-
temps et de l'automne. Il niche en Alaska
et au Yukon, et se rend hiverner au sud
du golfe du Mexique jusqu'en Argentine.

GENERAL CIGAR COMPANY, LIMITED, MONTREAL

Card 10

Life of
NELSON
ISSUED IN THE
Aristocratic
CIGARETTES.

Card 11

Card 12
These Pictures
are used in the

BRANDS OF CIGARETTES

Manufactured
by

CROWN TOBACCO CO

BOMBAY.

Card 13
Nº 9

FOOTBALL TEAMS OF THE BAILIWICK

BELGRAVES F.C. 2nd . XI.

F. Duquemin, W. Taylor (President), G. Staples,
L. Herivel, A. Taylor, J. Catts,
C. Elsbury (Committee), P. Osborne, W. J. Collins
(Hon. Sec.)
J. Collas, B. Tett, A. Rowe, A. Wellington, A. Thompson.

ISSUED WITH BUCKTROUTS' High Class Cigarettes

Card 14
WORLD FAMOUS

CINEMA ARTISTES

26

This is one of a
series of
pictures now being
packed with these
cigarettes.

HEDA HOPPER

METRO-GOLDWYN-MAYER

Card 15
"TURF"

VIRGINIA CIGARETTES

100% PURE

PERSONALITY SERIES
Footballers

No. 18
G. COVENTRY
(Collingwood)
Full Forward. The greatest
forward of modern times.
Has kicked more goals than
any forward playing. Holds
record of 18 goals in a match.
Has been playing with
Collingwood over twelve
years. A beautiful high mark
and long punt kick.

"TURF" CIGARETTES
CORK TIPPED & PLAIN
TURF FINE CUT

O. & CO.

Card 16
Nº 8

KEEP THIS CARD.
THE NUMBER ON IT MAY PROVE
OF ADVANTAGE TO YOU.

BUCKTROUT & Cº Lᵀᴰ

MANUFACTURERS OF
ALL THE FAMOUS
GUERNSEY-MADE CIGARETTES

THOMAS ALVA EDISON
was born at Milan, Ohio,
in 1847, and began life as a
railway newsboy. He
learned practical telegra-
phy, and soon applied himself to the improvement
of the system in vogue in
the United States. He
introduced the duplex,
triplex and multiplex me-
thods which he perfected
after he became Superin-
tendent of the New York
Gold and Stock Telegraph
Company. The Phono-
graph, Megaphone, and
Kinetoscope have all been
conceived and developed at
his home in New Jersey.

Card 17
ENGLISH PERIOD COSTUMES

No. 35

A Country Gentleman, 1780.

Various types of hat were worn
by the men of this period, ranging
from the tiny *chapeau bras* of the
dandies (*in size little larger than would
cover the muff-box of a beau*) to the
black broad-brimmed hats especially
affected by sportsmen. The semi-
military appearance of the costume
illustrated is due partly to the doubling
back of the front of the coat, and
partly to the black gaiters. These,
which had been worn by soldiers in
the early part of this century, became
generally fashionable later. Contem-
porary prints show that golf clubs
were longer (both in shaft and head)
than those of to-day; the golfer's
stance also was somewhat different.

A SERIES OF 50.

Card 18
INTERNATIONAL AIR LINERS

A SERIES OF 50

14

AIR FRANCE: POTEZ 62

(France)

The Potez 62 is a twin-engined,
high-wing passenger monoplane
with retractable undercarriage,
now in service on the lines of Air
France. In addition to the European services, they are being used
on the overland section of the
Paris-Saigon service, and on the
trans-Andean section of the South
American line to Santiago de
Chile. The main cabin is in two
sections, each section seating six
passengers. Fitted with two 1,000
h.p. Gnôme-Rhône K14 engines,
the Potez cruises at 175 m.p.h. It
weighs, fully loaded, 15,550 lbs.

Card 19
WONDERS OF THE SEA

A SERIES OF 50.

No. 18

The Giant Crab of Japan,
which resembles an enormous
spider.

The Giant Crab is in
natural forms is well shewn
the *Crustacea*—the great family
to which Crabs and Shrimps
belong. At one end of the
scale we have the tiny water-
fleas which are common in
ponds and ditches in England,
and which are under a hun-
dredth part of an inch in length.
At the other much larger
strange creature illustrated, the
Giant Crab of Japan, which is
probably the largest crab in
existence. Its nearly globular
body is over a foot across, and
the enormous claws sometimes
span as much as eleven feet.
The Giant Crab lives among
the weeds and rocks at the
bottom of the sea.

Card 20
(blank)

Card 21
NUMBER TWENTY-SEVEN

Cessna Airmaster

One of America's most efficient airplanes due largely to its very excel-
lent wing construction. Powered
with 165 h.p. Warner Super Scarab
engine this remarkable ship has top
speed at sea level of 169 m.p.h. at 8200
cruising speed of 151 m.p.h. at 8200
feet. Landing speed 49 m.p.h. Carries four passengers and has a
range of 725 miles.

This is one of a series of fifty pictures
of Modern American Airplanes
packed with
WINGS Cigarettes

Co-operation of *Popular Aviation Magazine*

Card 22
(blank)

Card 23
MODES OF CONVEYANCE

A SERIES OF 25

24

Turkey: Travelling
Carriage.

This quaint hearse-like wagon
has no glass windows. Lady
Mary Wortley Montagu wrote
from Adrianople in 1717: "These
Turkish coaches are not like
ours, but more convenient for
the country, the heat being so
great that glasses would be very
troublesome. They are made a
good deal in the manner of the
Dutch coaches, having wooden
lattices painted and gilded; the
inside being also painted with
baskets and nosegays of flowers,
intermixed commonly with little
poetical mottoes. They are
covered all over with scarlet
cloth, lined with silk, and very
often richly embroidered and
fringed. This covering entirely
hides the persons in them, but
may be thrown back at
pleasure, and the ladies peep
through the lattice. In the
summer they are almost entirely covered in the same manner." Closed Continental travelling is to be largely an uncom-
fortable experience.

BELGRAVES FOOTBALL CLUB 2nd XI.

AMREI.

ENGLISH PERIOD COSTUMES.

A COUNTRY GENTLEMAN, 1780.

THOMAS A. EDISON.

PHONOGRAPH.

G. COVENTRY

HEDA HOPPER

GIANT CRAB OF JAPAN.

AIR FRANCE: POTEZ 62

CESSNA "AIRMASTER"

COUSIS' CIGARETTES.

TURKEY: TRAVELLING CARRIAGE.

ELIZABETH YOUNG

12. RICCAREE BRAVE.

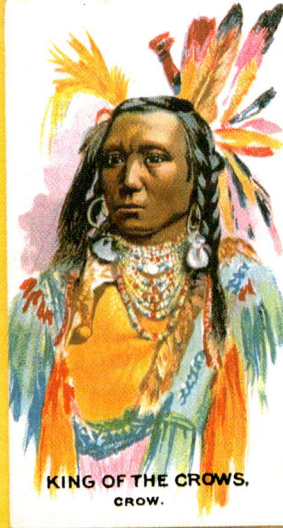

KING OF THE CROWS,
CROW.

SOUTHERN RAILWAY CO.

THE RED ADMIRAL.
(Pyrameis Atalanta)

STATE DAIMLER OF GEORGE VI

JAGUAR.

ENGLISHMAN.

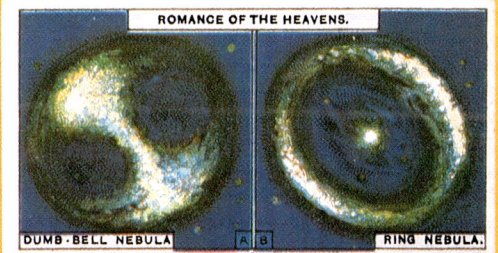

ROMANCE OF THE HEAVENS.

DUMB-BELL NEBULA   A B   RING NEBULA.

ENGINEERING WONDERS.

LETHBRIDGE VIADUCT.

2.   SUTCLIFFE

THE RHINOCEROS

Card 24

"TYPES" OF NORTH AMERICAN INDIANS

12. RICCAREE.

The close resemblance of the languages, proclaimed this tribe, undoubtedly, to be a part of the tribe of Pawnees: their personal appearance and customs were also very similar. Their locality was on the Platt River (R. Missouri), some hundreds of miles to the north of the Pawnees.

Card 25

CHARACTERS FROM THE WORKS OF CHARLES DICKENS

A SERIES OF 40.

No. 3

Uriah Heep.

Uriah Heep, the knavish and hypocritical clerk of Mr. Wickfield, typifies all that is cunning and treacherous. His outward fawning respect for "Mr. Copperfield" is assumed, in order to cloak his own malevolent ends. Mr. Micawber eventually exposes Heep's true character, and so brings about the failure of his deeply laid schemes.

Card 26

MODERN BEAUTIES

31

THIS IS ONE OF A SERIES OF 36 PHOTOGRAPHS NOW BEING PACKED WITH THESE CIGARETTES

FIRST SERIES

Card 27

THESE PICTURES are packed IN THE BRANDS OF CIGARETTES

MANUFACTURED BY

BRITISH-AMERICAN TOBACCO CO LTD.

Card 28

BUTTERFLIES

A SERIES OF...

The Red Admiral
Pyrameis Atalanta.

This conspicuous butterfly appears rather late in the Summer or early Autumn and may be seen wherever there are flowers or fruit, often flying in company with the Painted Lady both species being very fond of flying to the summits of hills. It has a wide range of Europe, North Africa, Northern and Western Asia, and North and Central America.

Card 29

SHIPS FLAGS & CAP BADGES

24 A SERIES OF 25

Southern Railway Co.,
London and Southampton.

This company has a large fleet of about 50 steamers with a gross tonnage of about 50,000. *Passenger and cargo services,* Southampton to Havre, to St. Malo and to Channel Islands, *summer passenger service,* Southampton to Caen; *cargo service only,* Southampton to Honfleur, and to Cherbourg. *Passenger and cargo services,* Newhaven to Dieppe, Dover to Calais, Dover to Boulogne, Folkestone to Boulogne, Portsmouth to Ryde, Lymington to Yarmouth, I. of W. During the Great War their faster vessels were taken over by the Admiralty as auxiliary cruisers, mine-layers and sweepers, despatch-boats, etc.

Card 30

INDIAN CHIEFS

4

This is one of a series of 50 pictures now being packed with these cigarettes

Card 31

TRANSPORT THEN & NOW

No. 48 STATE DAIMLER OF GEORGE VI (Present)

The Royal Car, seen in our picture, is a standard 4½ litre Daimler, with a special body by Hooper, with an engine of eight cylinders, giving a horse power of thirty-two. There is provision for full lighting in the interior for night riding in London, the arrangement being the Royal Standard on the roof on State occasions. The impression given by the car is one of power and luxury, coupled with dignity and restraint. See Edward VII's Daimler on No. 47.

THIS IS ONE OF A SERIES OF 48 CARDS NOW BEING PACKED WITH THESE CIGARETTES

Card 32

ROMANCE OF THE HEAVENS

A SERIES OF 50. 14

The Ring Nebula.

This well-known nebula is probably not actually ring-like, but consists of a more or less spherical "shell" of luminous gases surrounding the central star, the ring-like appearance being the result of the greater thickness of luminous matter in the line of sight.

The Dumb-bell Nebula.

This is one of the largest and the brightest of the planetary or ring-like nebulae. The central star of high temperature is surrounded by a more or less stationary "cloud" of luminous gas. It is thought that such nebulae originated in past outbursts of what are known as *novae,* or temporary stars.

Card 33

WORLD'S SMOKERS

ONE PACKED IN EACH BOX OF TEN CIGARETTES

Asiatic Turk	American
Austrian Soldier	African
Bulgarian	Albanian
Bavarian Hunter	Brazilian
Bavarian Postillion	Bedouin
Circassian	Cossack
Dutchman	Chinese
Dutchman (17th c'nty)	Farmer
Englishman	Greek
English Naval Officer	Gipsy
Gipsy Girl	Hindoo
Hungarian	Japanese
Indian (American)	Kalmuc
Old Planter	Mexican
Prussian officer of 1725	Morocco
Prussian Lieutenant	Odalisque
Russian Lady	Pole
Sir Walter Raleigh	Parisian
Swiss Cow-Keeper	Persian
Suabian Peasant	Student
Seydlitz Cuirassier	Spaniard
Swede (30 years' war)	Sailor
Soldier (Fr. Revolut'n)	Servian
Turkish Officer	Soudan
Thibet	Tyrolese

ALLEN & GINTER, RICHMOND, VIRGINIA.

Card 34

Wild Animals of the World

ONE PACKED IN EACH BOX OF CIGARETTES

Aard-vark,	Musk Ox,
Ant-eater,	Otter,
American Wild Cat,	Opossum,
American Elk,	Painted Ocelot,
Beaver,	Prong-horn Antelope,
Black Bear,	Polar Bean,
Buffalo,	Persian Gazelle,
Ghamois,	Porcupine,
Duck-billed Platypus,	Raccoon,
Dromedary,	Reindeer,
Eland,	Red Fox,
Elephant,	Rocky Mt. Sheep,
Grizzly Bear,	Stag,
Giant Kangaroo,	Sea Lion,
Giraffe,	Senegal Antelope,
Gorilla,	Tiger,
Hippopotamus,	Tapir,
Hyena,	Tasmanian Devil,
Ibex,	Virginian Deer,
Indian Rhinoceros,	Walrus,
Jaguar,	Wolf,
Leopard,	Wild Boar,
Lynx,	Yak,
Lion,	Zebu,
Monkey,	Zebra.

ALLEN & GINTER, RICHMOND-VIRGINIA.
GEO. S. HARRIS & SONS, LITH PHILA.

Card 35

ENGINEERING WONDERS

A SERIES OF 50

No. 2

(a) Bridge Construction. **Lethbridge Viaduct, Canada.**

Lethbridge, 759 miles west of Winnipeg, is the centre of an important coal mining district as well as of a large irrigation tract. Since the first steel track of the C.P.R. was laid across the Belly River, the track crossing the deep, wide ravine line has been made between Lethbridge and Mac-Leod. The most striking feature of this new piece of construction is the Lethbridge Viaduct which is over 5,327 ft. in length the maximum height of the railroad above the river bed being 314 ft. The track is carried upon 33 lattice steel towers, anchored upon concrete plinths supported upon concrete piles driven firmly into the silt.

Card 36

BIRDS, BEASTS AND FISHES.

31

Series of 50 Subjects.

The Rhinoceros is a native of Africa and Asia. There are several species, the Black Rhinoceros of Africa and the one-horned Indian Rhinoceros being best known. The hide is extremely thick, resembling armour in the case of the Indian variety. The horn is solid all through, not having a bony core as in the case of cattle.

Card 37

KONG BENG

Cigarettes

BRITISH AMERICAN TOBACCO Co Ltd.
ENGLAND

Card 38

ENGLISH CRICKETERS

Series of 25

NO. 2

SUTCLIFFE
Yorkshire.
Born November 25th, 1894.

Sutcliffe was England's best batsman during the Australian tour of 1924-25, breaking record for any one series of Tests by scoring 734 runs. His average was 81.55. He made four centuries in these Tests, getting 115, 176 and 127 in succession; the last two of these three equalled Bardsley's record at the Oval in 1909. He averaged 75.7 in Tests against S. Africa in 1924. Sutcliffe scored seven centuries for Yorkshire last season.

Card 39/63

Card 40

40

MASCOT

CIGARETTES

Card 41

41

THESE PICTURES are packed IN THE **BRANDS** OF **CIGARETTES** MANUFACTURED BY THE **AMERICAN TOBACCO CO.**

Card 42

42

BENSON & HEDGES (CANADA) LIMITED

Manufacturers of: Fabricants des:

Cigarettes "HENLEY" Cigarettes

These reproductions of ancient and modern fire fighting equipment are intended to emphasize the danger of fires. Save them for the youngsters, and make them fire conscious. | Ces reproductions d'appareils anciens et modernes contre les incendies sont émises dans le but d'appuyer sur les dangers du feu. Conservez-les pour les jeunes afin qu'ils soient toujours en garde contre le feu.

NO REDEEMABLE VALUE   AUCUNE VALEUR NEGOCIABLE

One tree will make a million matches—one match can destroy a million trees.

Card 43

43

BIRDS OF AMERICA
ONE PACKED IN EACH BOX OF
CIGARETTES

Albatross,	Meadow Lark,
Baltimore Oriole,	Mocking Bird,
Barn Swallow,	Mother Carey's Chicken,
Blue Bird,	Osprey,
Blue Bunting,	Pouter Pigeon,
Blue Jay,	Raven,
Bob-o-link,	Red Bird,
Cardinal Grosbeak,	Redstart,
Carolina Parrot,	Robin,
Carrier Pigeon,	Scarlet Tanager,
Catbird,	Sea Gull,
Chickadee,	Snow Bird,
Crossbill,	Snow Bunting,
Crow,	Snowy Owl,
Cuckoo,	Song Sparrow,
Dipper,	Starling,
Eagle,	Swallow-tailed Flycatcher,
Fantail Pigeon,	Swallow-tailed Hawk,
Goldfinch,	Tumbler Pigeon,
Great Northern Diver, (Loon,)	Whip-poor-will,
Horned Owl,	Woodpecker,
Humming Bird,	Wood Thrush,
Kingfisher,	Wood Warbler,
Magpie,	Wren,
Martin,	Yellow breasted Chat.

ALLEN & GINTER'S CIGARETTES
RICHMOND, VIRGINIA.

Card 44

44

THESE PICTURES

are packed

IN

BRANDS

OF

CIGARETTES

Manufactured

BY

THE **AMERICAN**

TOBACCO CO.

Card 45

45

AEROPLANES OF TODAY

A SERIES OF 50
SELECTED BY THE EDITOR OF "THE AEROPLANE"

5

AVRO "COMMODORE"
(Great Britain)

The "Commodore" is a small cabin biplane designed for the private owner or for the use of the air-travelling business man. It has a luxuriously furnished cabin with seating for four. The front seats are side by side and are fitted with dual controls; the two rear seats are situated so as to give the maximum amount of comfort. A seat for a fifth person may be added. The "Commodore" cruises at 110 m.p.h., and is a very pleasant machine to fly.

Card 46

46

Where did you get that hat?
Where did you get that tile?
Isn't it a nobby one,
And just the proper style?
I should like to have one
Just the same as that,
Where e'er I go, they shout: "Hello!
Where did you get that hat?"

COPYRIGHT, 1895 BY T. R. HARMS & CO. BY PERMISSION

THESE PICTURES ARE PACKED IN THE BRANDS OF CIGARETTES MANUFACTURED BY THE AMERICAN TOBACCO CO.

Card 47

47

THESE PICTURES are packed IN THE **BRANDS** OF **CIGARETTES** MANUFACTURED BY **BRITISH-AMERICAN TOBACCO CO LTD.**

Card 48/18

BRITISH BUTTERFLIES
A SERIES OF 50

18

LARGE COPPER.
(Chrysophanus dispar.)

This beautiful butterfly, now extinct, formerly occurred somewhat abundantly in the fens of Cambridgeshire, Huntingdonshire, Norfolk and Suffolk. The last authentic occurrence was the capture of five specimens near Holme, Hunts, in 1847 or 1848. In 1851 it was common in Whittlesea Mere, Cambs., but shortly afterwards rapidly decreased in number, and in the early forties it was rare. Its extinction was chiefly, if not solely, due to the burning and draining of the Fens when they were reclaimed. The sexes are very distinct in appearance, the female being partly barred and spotted with black. Wings expand 1¾ inches.

Card 49

49

EAGLE BIRD

CIGARETTES

MANUFACTURED BY
BRITISH-AMERICAN TOBACCO CO LTD
IN UNITED STATES OF AMERICA

Card 50

50

Cigarettes

Copain

Card 51

51

TIGER
CIGARETTES

10 CIGARETTES

TIGER
CIGARETTES

Card 52/43

No *Bears'* **43**

A SERIES OF 50

DO YOU KNOW
why a Scotsman wears a Sporran?

The early Scottish kilt was not a separate garment, but only the lower part of the plaid hanging down and arranged in folds below the belt. The word kilt (Danish *kilte*, to tuck up) is of Scandinavian origin, and means that which is "girded or tucked up." As there were no pockets in the Highlander's dress, the "Sporran" or "Spleuchan," a pocket-purse covered with fur, came into use. It was originally a simple receptacle or bag, made of goats' or badgers' skin, hung round the waist, but it is now a very ornamental affair with elaborate mountings, tassels, &c., and adds much to the distinctiveness of the Highlander's costume.

Number One Cigarettes

4 ♠ ♠

Paramount
CLAUDETTE COLBERT

MEXICO,
RURAL (GENDARME.)

Blue Jay.

ALLEN & GINTER
RICHMOND, VIRGINIA

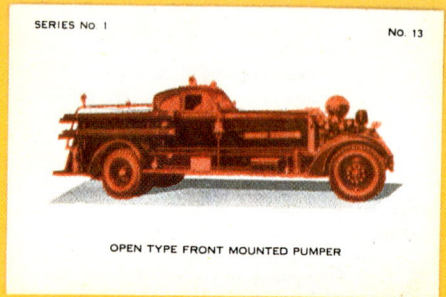

SERIES No. 1   NO. 13

OPEN TYPE FRONT MOUNTED PUMPER

G-ACNT

AVRO "COMMODORE"

Where did you get that Hat?

LARGE COPPER.

A SPORRAN.

8 ♣

A ♦

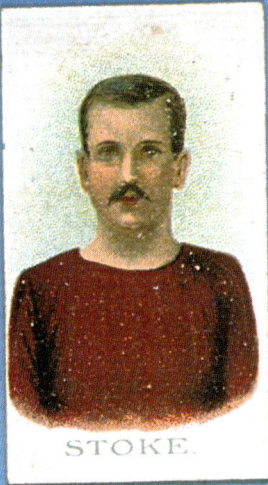

STOKE.

TURKEY.

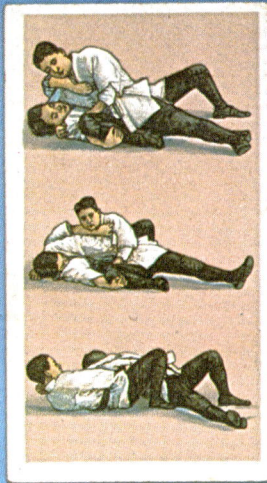

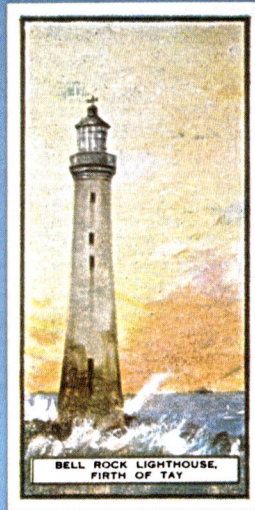

BELL ROCK LIGHTHOUSE,
FIRTH OF TAY

UNITED STATES of AMERICA. PRESIDENT

1ST BATTALION ESSEX REGIMENT.

REGIMENTAL COLOUR.   CAP BADGE.

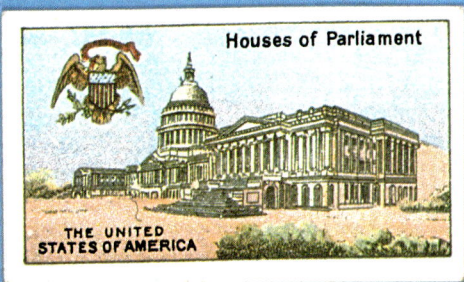

Houses of Parliament

THE UNITED
STATES OF AMERICA

SOUTH AFRICAN RAILWAYS.

S.S. EMPRESS OF SCOTLAND.

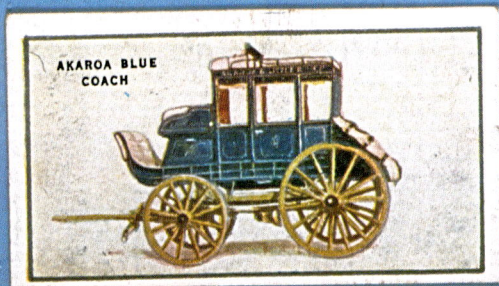

AKAROA BLUE
COACH

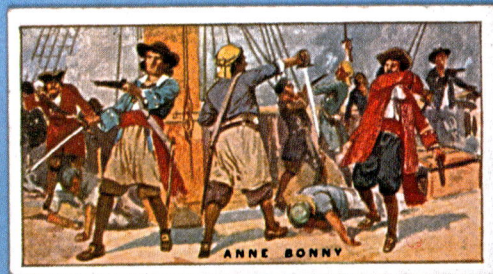

ANNE BONNY

"AQUITANIA."

WILLS'S CIGARETTES.

DRUM BANNER.   CAP BADGE.

18th (Princess of Wales's) Hussars.

Card 53

LIGHTHOUSES

40

53

Bell Rock Lighthouse.

This lighthouse was begun in 1807 under the super-intendence of Mr. Robert Stevenson. The execution of the work, attended as it was with exceptional difficulties, occupied four years, and the outlay was £61,331 9s. 2d. It was lit with oil and was about 108 feet from the sea level. The Bell Rock Light-house now exhibits a white and red light alternately. The tower is entirely solid up to a height of 30 feet.

The "Three Castles"

VIRGINIA CIGARETTES

W.D. & H.O. WILLS. BRISTOL & LONDON

Card 54

12

JIU-JITSU

(50 in Series)

54

Phase 1—This illustrates another way two antagonists may fall. The top man having his arm around opponent's neck his knee bearing on arm.

Phase 2—The under man should push knee against opponent's kidney, gripping coat collar and forcing chin back.

Phase 3—Continue the movement by pressing across throat until he surrenders.

Card 55

55

W.D. & H.O. WILLS

TRADE MARK

Bristol & London

WILLS's

Cigarettes

Card 56

56

SCISSORS

SPECIAL ARMY QUALITY

Card 57

REGIMENTAL STANDARDS AND CAP BADGES

A SERIES OF 50

57

56

1st Bn. The Essex Regiment.

This battalion is one of the few in the Army which still carries the old pattern big Colour. That illustrated is in very good condition, and has the spear-head top to the Colour-pike and no golden fringe to the Colour itself. In the Great War the Essex numbered 31 battalions, and gained 91 Battle Honours, the being—Le Cateau, Marne 1914, Ypres 1915 '17, Loos, Somme 1916 '18, Arras 1917 '18, Cambrai 1917 '18, Selle, Galli-poli 1915-16, and Gaza.

W.D. & H.O. WILLS

BRISTOL & LONDON

Card 58

58

WILLS's CIGARETTES.

W.D. & H.O. WILLS

TRADE MARK

Bristol & London

Card 59

RAILWAY ENGINES

A SERIES OF 50

59

36

South African Railways.

2-6-0-0-6-2 Mallet Compound Locomotive.

A very heavy and powerful compound locomotive of the articulated Mallet type, and used for hauling heavy coal trains. Has four cylinders, and is fitted with all the latest appliances, superheater, &c. An electric headlight is provided, and the engine can be worked simple or compound at will. Constructed for the 3' 6" gauge, and built in Scotland, the total weight of the engine and tender in working order is 179½ tons.

W.D. & H.O. WILLS

BRISTOL & LONDON

Card 60

60

Cigarettes

W.D. & H.O. WILLS
Bristol & London

Card 61

MERCHANT SHIPS OF THE WORLD

A SERIES OF 50

61

8

The "Empress of Scotland" is the largest liner in the service of the Canadian Pacific fleet, and has the distinction of being the largest steamer sailing between Europe and Canada. With a tonnage of 25,000, she is 677 feet in length, 17,500 indicated horse-power, and carries 465 first, 450 second, and 1,000 third class passengers. During the summer season she sails from Hamburg, Southampton, and Cherbourg, to Quebec, and dur-ing the winter season to St. John, New Brunswick.

W.D. & H.O. WILLS

BRISTOL & LONDON

Card 62

62

THIS SERIES CONSISTS OF 50 SUBJECTS.

BRITAIN'S DEFENDERS.

No. 36.

H.M.S. Queen.

One of the eight ships in the "Formidable" class, laid down during the years 1901 at Portsmouth, and com-pleted in 1902. She is now a unit of the Fifth Battle Squadron in the Home Fleet, commanded by Captain A. G. H. W. Napier, R.N. Length 420 feet, beam 75 feet. Displacement 15,000 tons. Main arma-ments, four 12 in., and twelve 6 in. guns.

Card 63

PIRATES & HIGHWAYMEN

A SERIES OF 25

63

4

Anne Bonny.

Anne Firing on the Men.

Born in County Cork, the daughter of an Attorney, Anne Bonny spent her girlhood in Carolina, where her father had settled. She ran away to sea with the famous pirate Capt. John Rackam ("Calico Jack"), and is said to have been as active as any of her male shipmates in boarding a prize. In Oct. 1720, the pirate ship was attacked by a sloop sent by the Governor of Jamaica. Anne Bonny and another woman named Mary Read, are said to have been the only members of the crew who made any resistance. In spite of their gallant defence, however, Rackam and his cowardly crew were captured and many of them executed.

W.D. & H.O. WILLS

BRISTOL & LONDON

Card 64

COACHES AND COACHING DAYS

A SERIES OF 50

64

39

Akaroa Blue Coach in the '90's.

This coach was imported from Concord, New Hampshire, U.S.A., by Mr. S. Lee, and was put together and finished in Christchurch. Unfortunately, to give it a neater appearance the axles were shortened, bringing the wheels closer to the body. This had the effect of making the vehicle heavy to pull. The inside was upholstered in red plush, and it was beautifully painted outside.

W.D. & H.O. WILLS

BRISTOL & LONDON

Card 65

65

UNITED SERVICE CIGARETTES.

W.D. & H.O. WILLS

BRISTOL & LONDON.

24

18TH PRINCESS OF WALES'S HUSSARS.

FIRST SERIES.

Card 66

66

SHIPS AND SHIPPING

SERIES OF 50 REAL PHOTOGRAPHS

27

AQUITANIA.

The oil burning, "Aqui-tania" is 901ft. long, 97ft. broad, 92ft. deep (from boat deck), and has a gross tonnage of 46,000. This steamer, engaged on the Southampton-New York service, comprises Louis XVI. restaurant, Elizabe-than grill room, Palladian Lounge, Carolean smoking room, Pompeian swimming bath, Adam drawing room, and library, and period suites and luxurious staterooms.

W.D. & H.O. WILLS

BRISTOL & LONDON

WILL'S CIGARETTES

LION.

ARCH OF SEPTIMIUS SEVERUS ROME.

PRIVATE S. F. GODLEY.

ATHENS P.M.
WHEN NOON AT GREENWICH 1HR 33 MINS. FAST.
Greece.
1 DRACHMA, VALUE 9½d
DIAMETER OF COIN. 29/32 INCH.

SUN

ALSATIAN WOLF DOGS.

BENTLEY

QUEENS WHARF, 1868

17. GREAT RAINBOW

37. POLAR BEAR "YOUNG SAM"

R.A.F. BOMBING PLANE IN ACTION.

WILL'S CIGARETTES.

WILL'S CIGARETTES.

FLAGS USED FOR FLAG SIGNALLING.

MEXICAN COWBOY.

VIOLETS

25

PLAYER'S CIGARETTES

BLOODHOUND.

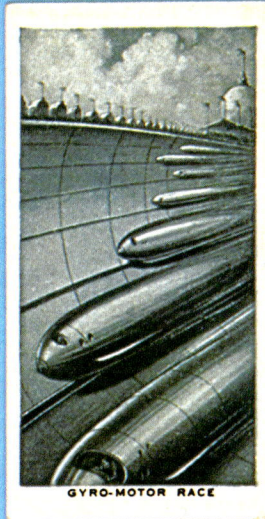

GYRO-MOTOR RACE

THE WALNUT.

INDIANA

COPYRT JS.

THE WHALE-BOAT.

MAY HALLOM.

PORTUGAL.

81

SOUTH AFRICAN SUCCULENTS

No. 21. CRASSULA RUPESTRIS.

This beautiful *Crassula* ranges from the west coast into the midlands of the Cape Province. It is often very abundant as bushy masses on northern slopes in the Karoo, where it produces exquisite effects of soft colour in its flowering season and throughout the year.

VETPLANTE.

No. 21. CRASSULA RUPESTRIS.

Hierdie pragtige *Crassula* word gevind van die westelike kus af tot in die middellande van die Kaap Provinsie. Dit vorm dikwels 'n bosagtige klomp aan die noordelike hange van die Karoo. Daar verskaf dit pragtige sagte kleure gedurende die blomtyd en ook deur die jaar.

FOR AN ALBUM SEND 6d. TO P.O. BOX 78, CAPE TOWN.
ISSUED BY THE WESTMINSTER TOBACCO CO. (C. T. & L.) LTD., LOWER COLLINGWOOD RD., OBSERVATORY, C.P.

C. T. LTD.

82

This is one of the series
"GARDEN FLOWERS OF THE WORLD"
50 in number
now being presented to smokers of
Westminster Cigarettes.

Westminster
Tobacco Co. Ltd, London.

83

POLO BRAND

OGDENS POLO CIGARETTES WITH MOUTHPIECES FINEST QUALITY

10

84

BRITISH TREES & THEIR USES

A SERIES OF 25

23

The Walnut.

(Juglans regia.)

A native of the Himalayas and of Asia Minor and Greece, the Walnut has been cultivated in Britain since the 15th century. It is a handsome tree, some 40-60 feet high, with a bole 20ft. in circumference, and bearing a profusion of large, fragrant leaves. In the familiar plum-like fruit the green flesh becomes brown and splits revealing the "stone" or Walnut. When young the fruits are used for pickling, while the ripe Walnuts are much appreciated for dessert (1 and 2). The tough, finely-figured wood, easily worked and capable of a beautiful polish, is used for furniture (3) and gun stocks (4).

Ogden's GUINEA GOLD CIGARETTES

85

THE WORLD OF TOMORROW

A SERIES OF FIFTY

34

GYRO-MOTOR RACE

A mechanized world need not lack in sporting excitement. Wherever speed is sought, whether for exploration, travel or war, there are records to be made and broken. Gyro-motor cars, such as those shown in our picture, would need specially-constructed tracks in which to race, so that they might attain speeds of hundreds of miles per hour without undue danger. Such events would be witnessed, not only by the crowds favoured with places along the sides of the track but, by means of television or a simultaneous cinema, by spectators all over the world. They would have more than a sporting interest; attempts to go "one better" would lead to improvements in design and a search for new inventions.

AN ATTRACTIVE ALBUM, PRICE ONE SHILLING, CAN BE OBTAINED FROM YOUR TOBACCONIST OR P.O. BOX 78, CAPE TOWN.

ISSUED BY THE WESTMINSTER TOBACCO CO. (C. T. & L.) LTD. LOWER COLLINGWOOD ROAD, OBSERVATORY, C.P.

HORTORS C.T.

86

DOGS

FROM PAINTINGS BY ARTHUR WARDLE

A SERIES OF 25

2

BLOODHOUND.

His acuteness of smell, and the intelligence and pertinacity with which he will keep to a scent and follow a trail, have made the Bloodhound invaluable in the pursuit of fugitives and in hunting—two services for which he was frequently employed in olden times. He is very powerful, with elastic and swinging gait, standing 25 to 27 inches high, and weighing about 110lbs.; bitches being 23 to 25ins., and weighing about 100lbs. The Bloodhound is affectionate and sensitive, and not at all quarrelsome. *Colours* tawny, black and tan, red and tan, sometimes flecked with white.

ISSUED BY

JOHN PLAYER & SONS

87

THESE PICTURES are packed IN THE BRANDS OF CIGARETTES made by MONOPOLY BUREAU of the IMPERIAL GOVERNMENT OF JAPAN MITSUI & CO. Sole Agents

---

88

JOHN PLAYER & SONS

WHALING

A SERIES OF 25

5

THE WHALE-BOAT.

The old-time whale-boat, which was some 27-35 feet long, was rowed by oars or fitted with a simple sprit-sail. Care had to be taken to keep every article in its place, for the slightest mistake would have endangered the lives of all in the boat. At the bow were two harpoons and two or three lances, while lines of the finest hemp, 200 or 300 fathoms long, were coiled in wooden tubs. A deep slot in the bow received the line and a *logger-head* was fixed, around which the line was turned. In the forward thwart was the *knee-brace* or clumsy cleat to steady the left thigh of the harpooner. The rowlocks were greased and padded to render the rowing as silent as possible.

89

Le Roy LITTLE CIGARS L. MILLER & SONS. N.Y.U.S.A.

INDIANA, B. S.

Captain, H. C. Taylor.
Keel Laid, 1891.
Displacement, 10,288 tons.
Speed, 15.54 knots.
Horse Power, 9,738.
Cost, $3,020,000.
Main Battery, 4-13, 8-8, 4-6 in.
Length, 348 ft., Breadth, 69 ft.,
Depth, 24 ft.
Coal Capacity, 1,640 tons.
Officers, 38; Men, 427.

90

SMOKE PLAYER'S NAVY MIXTURE

John Player & Sons ENGLAND.

91

"HAWAGHARRI"

PENINSULAR TOBACCO CO. LTD MONGHYR, INDIA.

CIGARETTES & MOUTHPIECES PENINSULAR TOBACCO CO. LTD MONGHYR, INDIA

92

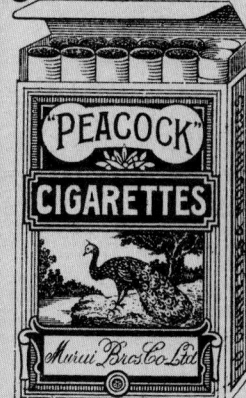

"PEACOCK" CIGARETTES

Murai Bros. Co. Ltd.

93

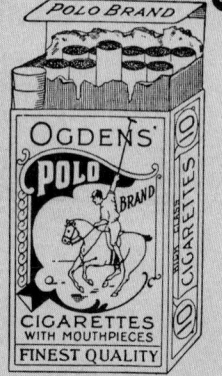

POLO BRAND

OGDENS POLO CIGARETTES WITH MOUTHPIECES FINEST QUALITY

10

94

BETWEEN THE ACTS

The Manufacture of Cigarettes

NEW YORK

G. W. GAIL & AX

95

Arms of Dominions

GIVEN WITH EACH BOX OF

WM. S. KIMBALL & CO.'S
CIGARETTES:

ALSACE	ITALY
ARGENTINE REP.	MODENA
AUSTRIA	MONACO
BADEN	NAPLES
BAVARIA	NEW GRENADA
BELGIUM	PARAGUAY
BRAZIL	PORTUGAL
CHILI	PRUSSIA
COSTA RICA	ROMAN PONTIFF
DENMARK	RUSSIA
ECJADOR	SARDINIA
LN LAND	SAVOY
„ PR. OF WALES	SAXONY
FRANCE KINGDOM	SCOTLAND
„ EMPIRE	SPAIN
„ BOURBON	„ CASTILE
„ ORLEANS	„ LEON
„ BURGUNDY	SWEDEN
GREECE	TURKEY
GUATEMALA	TUSCANY
HANOVER	„ MEDICI
HAYTI	TWO SICILIES
HESSE-DARMSTADT	U. S. COLUMBIA
HOLLAND	WURTEMBURG

96

Butterflies of the World.

PACKED ONLY WITH

KINNEY BROS.' HIGH CLASS
CIGARETTES.

THIS COLLECTION OF BUTTERFLIES IS SELECTED FROM THE MOST BEAUTIFUL TO BE FOUND ON THE GLOBE.

THE FIFTY, PROPERLY PLACED FORM A HANDSOME BANNER. A KEY, OR PLAN TO ASSIST IN ARRANGING THE CARDS, WILL BE SENT FOR SEVEN TICKETS, OR, IF DESIRED, THE BANNER, WITHOUT ANY ADVERTISEMENT ON IT, WILL BE SENT FOR FIFTY TICKETS. THESE CARDS CAN BE RETAINED.

ONLY OUR TICKETS RECEIVED

97

BUTTERFLIES
GIVEN WITH EACH BOX OF

WM. S. KIMBALL & CO.
CIGARETTES

1 GYNAECIA DIRCE	26 ARGYNNIS CYBELE
2 MORPHO TEUCER	27 PARNASSIUS APOLLO
3 GRAPTA GRACILIS	28 TERIAS LISA
4 VANESSA MILBERTI	29 HELICONIA CYDNO
5 DANAIS ARCHIPPUS	30 PYRAMEIS ATALANTA
6 CALIMORPHA HERA	31 RHODOCERA CLEOPATRA
7 GRAPTA INTERROGATIONIS	32 PYRAMEIS CARYAE
8 LIMENITIS URSULA	33 PAPILIO PODALIRIUS
9 LIMENITIS ARTHEMIS	34 PIERIS BRASSICAE
10 GRAPTA COMMA	35 LIMENITIS SYBILLA
11 MELITAEA PHAETON	36 JUNONIA LAVINIA
12 VANESSA URTICAE	37 CATOCALA NUPTA
13 PAPILIO TURNUS	38 CHRYSOPHANUS AMERICANUS
14 PAPILIO CRESPHONTES	39 THECLA SMILACIS
15 PYRAMEIS TAMMEAMEA	40 PYRAMEIS HUNTERA
16 VANESSA IO	41 CHRYSOPHANUS THOE
17 MELITAEA NYCTEIS	42 ARGYNNIS IDALIA
18 PAPILIO MACHAON	43 VANESSA ANTIOPA
19 ARGYNNIS AGLAJA	44 PAPILIO PHILENOR
20 PYRAMEIS CARDUI	45 URANIA RHIPHEUS
21 LIMENITIS DISIPPUS	46 MORPHO MENELAUS
22 CATOCALA FRAXINI	47 ORNITHOPTERA BROOKIANA
23 AGLIA TAU	48 MORPHO CYPRIS
24 PAPILIO HIPPODAMUS	49 PREPONA AMPHIMACHUS
25 VANESSA J. ALBUM	50 PLATYSAMIA CECROPIA

JULIUS BIEN & CO. LITH. N.Y.

98

RAILWAY WORKING
SERIES OF 50

41

Snow Plough.

While snow does not present to the British railway engineer the difficulties which it does in America and elsewhere, its occasional visits can prove extremely inconvenient all the same! The Northern and Scottish lines receive the brunt of what we do get, and we show here two ways of dealing with it. In the top one a plough is used on the North-Eastern section of the L. & N.E.R., consisting of two ploughs in one, a double-ended unit. In heavy drifts the usual rule is to "charge" into the obstruction, and gradually to make a passage through.

JOHN PLAYER & SONS
NOTTINGHAM, ENGLAND.

99

Prominent People

No. 52

Scerri's

High Class

Cigarettes

100

POPULAR FILM STARS

35

This Real Photograph is one of a series of
50
now being packed with these cigarettes

LAMBERT & BUTLER
ENGLAND

101

MOTOR CARS
A SERIES OF 56

49
STAR

"The creation of the Star Car is the most important and brilliant accomplishment of any undertaking identified with the automobile industry.

Smartness in looks, sturdiness and modern design throughout, and a refinement of construction in a lower price field were unheard of until the Star was created by W. C. Durant.

The "New Series" Star Car has all the advantages of the old. There is ample proof of performance ability. Although introduced only last year, the original Star Car has demonstrated its merits in the service of over 120,000 owners all over the world.

ISSUED BY
IMPERIAL TOBACCO Co
OF CANADA LTD.
MONTREAL.

17507

102

INDIAN HISTORICAL VIEWS
No. 7
A Series of 25

RAILWAY
CIGARETTES

THE IMPERIAL TOBACCO Co OF INDIA Ltd.
Successors in India to
BRITISH-AMERICAN TOBACCO Co Ltd

103

VICTORIA CROSS HEROES
SERIES OF 25.
No 8.

Lance-Corporal Fuller, 2nd Batt. Welsh Regiment.

The great bravery exhibited by this regiment is typified in the gallant conduct of Lance-Corporal William Fuller, who won his V.C. near Chivy-sur-Aisne, on Sept. 14, 1914. He advanced a hundred yards under heavy machine-gun and rifle fire to rescue Captain Haggard, who lay on the field mortally wounded, and carried him back to cover.

104

PUGILISTS IN ACTION
A SERIES OF 50

No. 3

"Drumhead"
CIGARETTES

JOHN PLAYER & SONS
ENGLAND

105

TRADE T&B MARK

CIGARETTES

MANUFACTURED
OF THE FINEST
VIRGINIA TOBACCO

The Geo. E. Tuckett
& Son Co. Ltd.
HAMILTON, ONT. CANADA

106

Kinney Bros
NOVELTIES. 50 STYLES.
ONE IN EACH PACKAGE OF
CIGARETTES

107

KINNEY TOBACCO Co
NEW YORK, RICHMOND, BALTIMORE, DANVILLE.
SUCCESSOR TO
Kinney Bros.

SURF BEAUTIES
ONE PACKED IN EACH BOX OF
AMERICAN
CIGARETTES

AMERICAN	FOREIGN
NEWPORT	RAMSGATE
LONG BRANCH	SCARBOROUGH
NARRAGANSETT	BRIGHTON
ISLE OF SHOALS	TORQUAY
BLOCK ISLAND	CHERBOURG
FIRE ISLAND	DIEPPE
ROCKAWAY	OSTENDE
NANTASKET	TROUVILLE
NANTUCKET	BOULOGNE
BAR HARBOR	ST. MICHEL
ATLANTIC CITY	PARAME
CAPE MAY	ST MALO
WATCH HILL	DINARD
OLD ORCHARD BEACH	GRANVILLE
LONG BEACH	CREVE DAZETTE
NAHANT	LIVORNO
DEAL BEACH	CAIS
SEA GIRT	ST JUAC
SWAMPSCOTT	ENOGAT
COHASSET	MT ST. MICHEL
MONTEREY	ST ENOGAT
SANTA BARBARA	ST BRELADE
ASBURY PARK	VAL ANDRE
OLD POINT COMFORT	ST CLEMENT

108

WHO'S WHO IN SPORT (1926)
A SERIES OF 50

30

JACK HOBBS

John Berry Hobbs, whose powers seem to grow greater as his age increases, was born at Cambridge in 1882, and first played in first-class cricket for Surrey against Essex in 1905. Since then he made 155. Since then he has scored 138 other centuries, and in addition to proving a tower of strength to Surrey, has been England's leading batsman for many years.

LAMBERT & BUTLER
ENGLAND.

36 Chrysophanus americanus

COSTA RICA

BETWEEN THE ACTS & BRAVO CIGARETTES.

WM. HENRY HARRISON.
PREST U.S. 1841, 1 MONTH.

35 RUDOLPH VALENTINO

ROB. BURNS.

SNOW - PLOUGH.

STAR

ALF BARBER.

LANCE CORPORAL FULLER.

The Khas Mahal. Agra

36. J. HOBBS

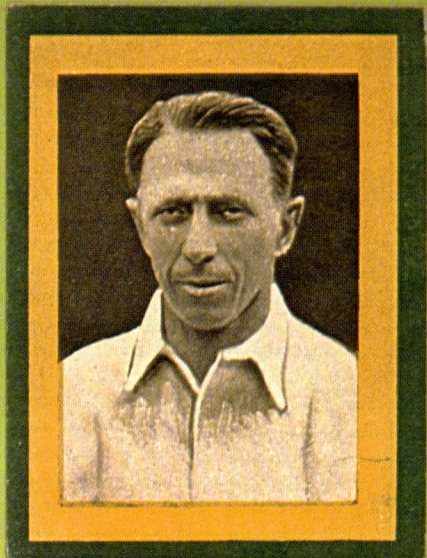

ARMS OF
SALISBURY
RHODESIA

DISCRIMINE SALUS

SLAVE DHOW

COLOURED SANDS, ALUM BAY, I.O.W.

SPARTAN "CRUISER"

Officer, Black Watch, 1912

BENGAL LANCERS

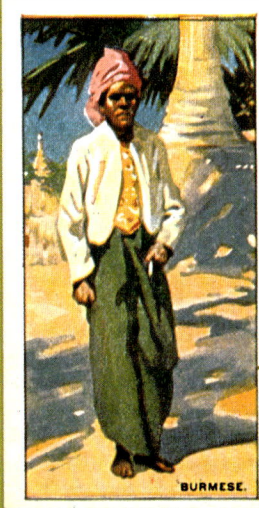

BURMESE.

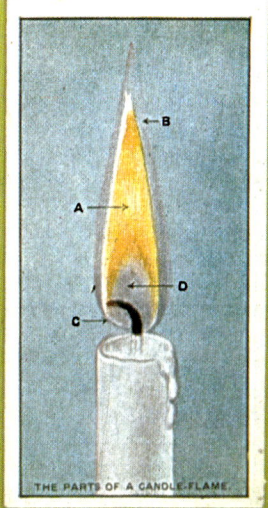

THE PARTS OF A CANDLE-FLAME.

109

SPRINGBOK RUGBY & CRICKET TEAMS 1931

A SERIES OF 47.   No. 36.

H. W. TAYLOR.

Now in his 42nd year, Herby Taylor is well known to the whole cricketing world. As long ago as 1914, he was considered the best batsman this country had then produced, and since that time no player has seriously challenged his right to that title.

Taylor has scored more runs in Currie Cup and Test cricket than any other South African, and between 1913 and 1924 he captained South Africa in twenty consecutive Test matches against England and Australia. In Test matches against both countries Taylor has played 65 innings and scored 2,613 runs. In the recent Tests against England he scored 299 in 7 innings.

Taylor's strong point is his marvellous footwork and strong back play. On the on-side he is excelled by few, and in his youth his accurate and daring pull-shots were a brilliant feature of his play.

ISSUED BY
THE UNITED TOBACCO COS. (SOUTH) LTD.
CAPE TOWN.

110

OUR SOUTH AFRICAN BIRDS
ONS SUID-AFRIKAANSE VOËLS

GURNEY'S SUGAR-BIRD

ROOIBORS-SUIKERVOEL

Promerops gurneyi

A handsome volume edited by the Curator of the Bird and Mammal Collections, Transvaal Museum, to contain these pictures is obtainable, price 3d., from your tobacconist, providing stocks are available.

'n Pragtige bundel, onder redaksie van die Kurator van die Voël en Soog dier Versamelings, Transvaal Museum, waarin hierdie pictures geplak kan word, is teen 3d. by u tabakhandelaar verkrygbaar, mits voorraad voorhande is.

N SERIES OF 100 NOW BEING PACKED WITH THESE CIGARETTES
'N REEKS VAN 100 WORD NOU MET HIERDIE SIGARETTE VERPAK

C.T.LTD.

111

OUR SOUTH AFRICAN FLORA

AGAPANTHUS
(No. 5.)
AGAPANTHUS
(*Agapanthus umbellatus*)

A handsome volume edited by the Director of the National Botanic Gardens, Kirstenbosch, Cape Town, to contain these pictures is obtainable, price 3d., from your tobacconist.

'n Pragtige bundel, onder redaksie van die Kurator van die Nasionale Botaniese Tuin, Kirstenbosch, Kaapstad, waarin hierdie prentjies geplak kan word, is teen 3d. by u tabakhandelaar verkrygbaar.

SERIES OF 100 NOW BEING PACKED WITH THESE CIGARETTES
'N REEKS VAN 100 WORD NOU MET HIERDIE SIGARETTE VERPAK

C.T. LTD.

112

SOUTH AFRICAN BUTTERFLIES

FROM THE DRAWINGS BY S. W. TWINE.

A series of 52 now being packed with SPRINGBOK CIGARETTE

'n Reeks van 52 wat nou verpak word met SPRINGBOK-SIGARETTE

5. THE TWILIGHT BROWN.
(*Melanitis leda.*)

A most extraordinarily variable butterfly, in shape, colouring and markings. Very widely spread in Africa, Asia and Australia. Hides in dark, shady spots in woods during day and emerges in evening, to flit about until after dark. Caterpillar is yellow with green stripes and feeds on grass : it has two horns on its head. December to March. Reduced.

5. DIE SKEMER-BRUINE.
(*Melanitis leda.*)

'n Buitengewoon veranderlike skoenlapper wat betref fatsoen, kleur en merke. Baie wyd verspreid in Afrika, Asie en Australie. Skuil in donker, skaduryke plekke in die bos gedurende die dag en kom in die aand te voorskyn, wanneer hy rond- vlieg totdat dit donker is. Die ruspe is geel met groen strepe en eet gras : het twee horinkies op sy kop. Desember tot Maart. Verklein.

Issued by The United Tobacco Cos (South) Ltd.,
32. Kloof Street, Cape Town.

C.T. LTD.

113

SOUTH AFRICAN COATS OF ARMS
A SERIES OF 52

No. 24.

SALISBURY

Salisbury is the capital and the seat of the Government of Rhodesia. It is the centre of the maize and tobacco industries, and of a rich gold mining district. It is also the social centre, and is well laid out with broad thoroughfares and shady avenues.

The Government offices are erected on the spot from where the pioneers, who had opened up the country, were disbanded in 1890. The lower left hand quarter of the shield in the Coat of Arms contains the old Cape Colony Arms, and the crest denotes the mining and agricultural pursuits of the district.

Population (1929) : Europeans, 7324.

ISSUED BY
THE UNITED TOBACCO COS. (SOUTH) LTD.
CAPE TOWN

114

THE STORY OF SAND

24

(Sand in Nature).

COLOURED SANDS, ALUM BAY, I.O.W.

These famous cliffs consist of variously coloured sands and clays laid down in what geologists term the Eocene (i.e., "New Dawn") period, in which life as we know it, emerged. Conditions were tropical, for the leaf- beds show that palms and figs grew among the oaks, while crocodiles and turtles lived in the waters. The brilliant and varied sands of Alum Bay, which are rendered very conspicuous by the almost vertical position of the strata, are best seen after a storm of rain. We show one of the glass orna- ments, familiar to visitors to the Isle of Wight, in which the contrasting colours of the sands are well displayed.

A SERIES OF 50 NOW BEING PACKED WITH THESE CIGARETTES

115

SHIPS OF ALL TIMES

No. 15.

THE DHOW.

The *dhow* is a type of vessel used throughout the Arabian Sea. The language to which the word belongs is unknown, but the term is used of any native craft along the East African coast having a burden of between 150 and 200 tons, and a stem rising in a long slope from the water. *Dhows* generally have one mast with a lateen sail, the yard being enormously long. Much of the trade of the Red Sea and Persian Gulf is carried on by these vessels, which were formerly regularly employed in the slave trade from the East Coast of Africa.

A series of 40 subjects now being packed with these cigarettes

116

WILD ANIMALS OF THE WORLD

No. 24.

THE OUNCE.

The Snow-Leopard, as the Ounce is often called, is noteworthy as being the only one of the "Great Cats" which is confined to tem- perate and cold climates. This ani- mal is only found in the heights of the Himalayas and Central Asiatic ranges. In disposition, the Ounce appears harmless enough, as it has never been known to attack human beings; although said to be as fierce as the Leopard regarding other animals. The ordinary prey of the Snow-Leopard are wild goats and sheep. It is also a destructive foe to tame goats and sheep and even ponies fall victims.

A series of 50

117

AEROPLANES OF TO-DAY

A SERIES OF FIFTY SELECTED BY THE EDITOR OF "THE AEROPLANE"

22

SPARTAN "CRUISER"
(Great Britain)

The Spartan "Cruiser" seen here flying off the coast of the Isle of Wight is one of a fleet of three-engined, six-eight-seater mono- planes which carry passengers on a daily service between London and the Isle of Wight. The three engines provide a margin of safety in the event of a single or double engine failure and the three together ensure a comfortable cruising speed of 115 m.p.h. Spartan "Cruisers" are used in various parts of the world for short-distance air lines and special charter work. During 1933 one of these fleet, a party to Australia and back, with deviations on the route making up a total mileage of 32,000

FOR AN ALBUM SEND 6d TO BOX 78 CAPE TOWN

118

INTERESTING EXPERIMENTS
SERIES OF 25

10

The Parts of a Candle- Flame.

When we light the wick of a Candle the heat causes the wax to melt, and the resulting liquid is drawn up the wick by capillary attraction. On reaching the top it is turned into inflammable Hydrocarbon vapour. The actual Flame produced consists of three parts : (a) the brightly luminous area ; (b) the faintly luminous outer area ; and (c) the non-luminous area at the base. These three parts enclose the dark inner cone (b), which consists of heated unburnt gases, and is therefore not part of the actual Flame.

ISSUED BY
THE UNITED TOBACCO COS.(SOUTH) LTD.

119

PICTURESQUE PEOPLE OF THE EMPIRE
A SERIES OF 25

8

Burmese.

The Burmese live in a land teeming with vegetation, where almost anything will grow. As nature has provided them with most of their requirements, with but little exertion on their part, they are perhaps rather inclined to indolence. Good-natured and easy-going, gay and lively, the Burmese have been termed " the Irish of the East." They are brown, but never very dark, with rather coarse black hair. Bur- mese men are unable to compete with the Chinese, Japanese and Hindus who settle in their coun- try ; the women, however, have keener business instincts and carry on much of the internal trade of Burma.

ISSUED BY
THE UNITED TOBACCO COS. (SOUTH) LTD.
CAPE TOWN.

120

A SERIES OF 50

Bengal Lancer.

NO. 11

The Indian Trooper is generally of a high caste, whose creed prohibits him from engaging in trade or any menial occupation—he often has native servants in attendance. A soldier's life is a natural career to him, as he is descended from genera- tions of fighting ancestors.

In many things as horse- men the Indian Cavalry can give points to our British Troopers, but in actual fighting they cannot stand so well the shock of combat.

RIDERS OF THE WORLD

THE UNITED TOBACCO CO's (SOUTH) LTD.

121

REGIMENTAL UNIFORMS

A SERIES OF 50 NOW BEING PACKED WITH THESE CIGARETTES

38

Black Watch, No. 4.

Officer, The Royal Highlanders, Black Watch, 1912.

The old 42nd can be distin- guished from the other High- land regiments by the red hackle feather worn in the bonnet. The Black Watch took a gallant part in the war in South Africa, and at Magers- fontein in 1899 they lost 19 officers and over 300 men killed and wounded.

FOR AN ALBUM SEND 6d. TO
P.O. Box 1004, Cape Town

C.T.LTD.

122

THESE PICTURES ARE PACKED IN THE BOXES OF

NAILERS Cigarettes

SOLE AGENTS, The Planters' Stores & Agency Co Ltd., CALCUTTA.

K426.

123

ARMS & ARMOUR.

A Series of 50.

27

A Footsoldier with a Hand-Gun.

Although firearms were invented in the early part of the 14th century, they had at first little influence in military operations. The hand-gun of this period consisted of a tube of iron or brass, and was fixed to a straight wooden stock. The touch-hole was at the top of the barrel, there being no lock of any kind. The early hand-gun was fired by means of a lighted match held in the hand.

124

40

BEAUTIFUL NEW ZEALAND

A SERIES OF 50 REAL PHOTOGRAPHS

Maori Chief (1).

This tattooed warrior of the northern tribes is a typical specimen of the fighting man that first greeted the European settlers. Hardy warriors of a fearless breed, these Maori braves fought the British soldiers during the Maori Wars with a valour and determination that won the lasting respect of their opponents. Now they are a peaceful, well educated race, proud to be citizens of the British Empire.

BY COURTESY OF THE NEW ZEALAND GOVERNMENT PUBLICITY OFFICE.

THREE CASTLES VIRGINIA CIGARETTES

W.D. & H.O. WILLS. BRISTOL & LONDON.

125

126

ISSUED BY W. D. & H. O. WILLS (N.Z.) LTD. IN SUPPORT OF NEW ZEALAND'S ROAD SAFETY CAMPAIGN.

SAFETY FIRST

A SERIES OF 50

43.—LOOK BEFORE YOU LEAVE THE PAVEMENT

Before stepping off the pavement look towards the oncoming traffic to assure yourself that it is safe to cross. Do not make a sudden dash into the roadway, especially with your back to the traffic. When walking near the edge of the pavement it is best to face the oncoming traffic, for heavy vehicles travelling slowly near the road edge sometimes have loads that slightly overhang the footpath. Take special care if you have to step out behind or in front of any vehicle or other obstruction which prevents a clear view of the road.

CAPSTAN NAVY CUT CIGARETTES

ALBUMS AT ALL TOBACCONISTS

127

P. O. Curran.
Born 1882.
Height 5 ft. 10½ in.
Weight 14 st.
Best performance.
Beat Gunner Moir in 2 rounds at Mountain Ash May 23rd 1910.

128

W.D. & H.O. WILLS Bristol & London TRADE MARK

WILL'S Cigarettes

129

CRICKET SEASON 1928-29

THIS REAL PHOTOGRAPH IS ONE OF A SERIES OF ENGLISH & AUSTRALIAN CRICKETERS.

W.D. & H.O. WILLS

TRADE MARK

130

OPEN HERE

PURPLE MOUNTAIN Cigarettes

131

A SERIES OF AUSTRALIAN AND ENGLISH CRICKETERS

THIS PICTURE IS THE No 12 OF A SERIES OF PROMINENT AUSTRALIAN AND ENGLISH CRICKETERS

"CAPSTAN" NAVY CUT

FOR PIPE SMOKERS IS UNEQUALLED ALSO OBTAINABLE IN PLUG FORM

ALBUMS FOR THESE PICTURE CARDS CAN BE OBTAINED AT 1/- EACH THROUGH ALL TOBACCONISTS

132

OGDENS RULER CIGARETTES

133

"PIRATE"

Cigarettes.

W.D. & H.O. WILLS Bristol & London

134

CHILDREN OF ALL NATIONS

A SERIES OF 50

30 NEW ZEALAND.

The Maoris of New Zealand are now restricted to North Island and the north of South Island. Their dress consists of a long mat of the fibres of New Zealand flax, dyed in various colours; while the chiefs wear cloaks of feathers or skins. Maori boys and girls enjoy playing such games as cat's cradle, giant's stride, skipping, hide-and-seek, and many singing games; while older youths and maidens love to dance the *Haka*, a dance accompanied by singing.

PUSH

W.D. & H.O. WILLS BRISTOL & LONDON

135

THIS SERIES CONSISTS OF 28 SUBJECTS

SCISSORS CIGARETTES

SPECIAL ARMY QUALITY

W.D. & H.O. WILLS BRISTOL & LONDON

No 12

136

SCISSORS CIGARETTES W.D. H.O. WILLS BRISTOL & LONDON

SPECIAL ARMY QUALITY

137

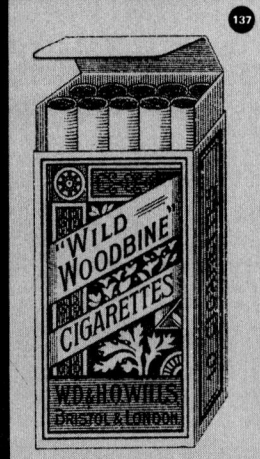

WILD WOODBINE CIGARETTES

W.D. & H.O. WILLS BRISTOL & LONDON

40. MAORI CHIEF (1)

WILLS'S CIGARETTES.

1485.
Time of Battle of Bosworth.

MADAME CALVE.

NAILERS Cigarettes.

E. TYLDESLEY, LANCS

DANISH POLICE.

P. O. CURPAN,
British

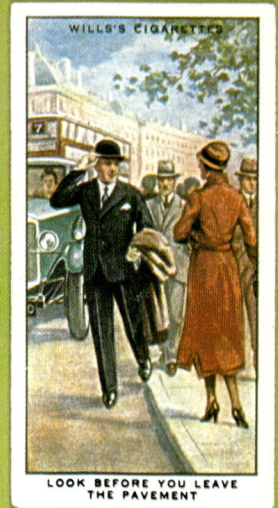

WILLS'S CIGARETTES

LOOK BEFORE YOU LEAVE
THE PAVEMENT

"WILLS'S"
CIGARETTES.

T. J. MATTHEWS,
VICTORIA.

BRITISH ARMY UNIFORMS.

No 40

DRUM HORSE OF THE
3rd, King's Own Hussars.

INDIA

NEW ZEALAND.

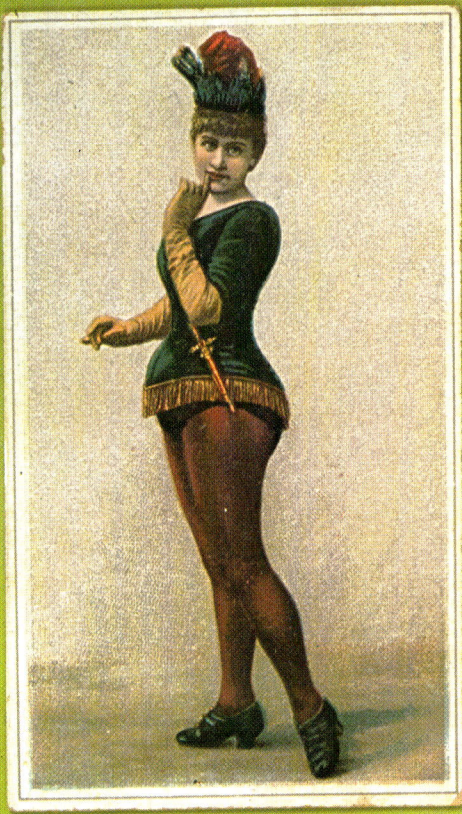

HURDLING THE CORRAL

L'Imtarfa   E. A. Gouder

GIANTS

Otis Crandall
OF THE
NEW YORK NATIONALS

SLAGLE, BALTIMORE.

THE MAORI.

PARTRIDGE COCHIN HEN.

Card 159

DO YOU KNOW ?

No. 9

The most perfect
building in the world

The Taj Mahal at Agra in India,
built almost entirely of
dazzling-white marble, is considered by many people to be
the most perfect building in
the world. It certainly pro-
vides an unforgettable sight
to its many visitors. It was
built in 1650 and dedicated by
Shah Jehan to the memory of
his wife, Mumtaz-i-Mahal.
Both are buried here.

Card 160

INDIAN LIFE IN THE "60'S"

THE SCENT OF
TOBACCO

The Indian power of sight and smell is
wonderful. They will scent the tobacco or
coffee in a camp for many miles and have
been known to find their way to a camp
by this means.

Card 161

SHIPS
AND THEIR
WORKINGS

No. 11
DUAL PURPOSE
CAR FERRY

This new ferry can carry 45
cars or lorries and their
passengers, and is also used as
a passenger ferry for 1,200
people. The cars run up a
ramp onto a turntable and
then down the other side.
No. 1, approach ramp : No. 2,
floating mooring pontoon :
No. 3, fixed mooring posts.

Card 162

**LES PRODUITS
DU MONDE**
UNE SERIE DE 25

1
Les Etats Unis D'Amerique
Le Tabac

Le tabac fut un des trésors du
Nouveau Monde que Sir Walter
Raleigh et d'autres explorateurs
introduisirent en Europe. De
nos jours, les plus grandes plan-
tations de tabac du monde se
trouvent encore aux Etats Unis,
les plus importants centres pro-
ducteurs étant le Tennessee, la
Virginie, la Caroline du Nord et
le Kentucky. Les meilleures
cigarettes, comme la "Domino",
sont faites dans des usines
modernes avec du tabac
sélectionné.

Card 163

Card 164

HYENA

These animals are of
two varieties. The lar-
gest is a
is a or or
native of Africa. They
are ugly in appearance,
and their habits noc-
turnal and loathsome.

Card 165

Card 166

THE
WORLD of SPORT
A SERIES OF 100.

54
WALTER LINDRUM
(Australia)

Age 36. Greatest Billiards player of the
day. Plays left-handed. Made his first
1,000 break when 17 years of age. Holds
record of highest break of 4,137. Winner
of the World's Championship at Melbourne in 1934, with score of 23,553.

WALTER LINDRUM
(Australië)

Ouderdom 36. Grootste Biljartspeler van
sy tyd. Is 'n links speler. Het sy eerste
1,000-seriestoot op 17-jarige leeftyd
gemaak. Is in besit van die rekord van
die hoogste seriestoot van 4,137. Wenner
van die Wêreldkampioenskap te Melbourne in 1934, met 'n telling van 23,553.

Card 167

Card 168

168

Card 169

Poppy — Consolation.

In the 16th century the village
Damons and Phyllises proved
the sincerity of lovers by placing
a petal of the poppy in the palm
of the left hand, which, on being
struck by the other hand, gave a
sound that denoted true attach-
ment.

Card 170

Card 171

ON THE SCENT OF TOBACCO

COPYRIGHTED 1910 BY AMER TOB CO.

35

Hyena

O. Bilancia

Nº10

MORGAN QUINN, SHAMROCK TEAM

"TRIERE" OLD GREEK WAR
SHIP AT THE BATTLE OF
"SALAMIS" 480 B.C.

JOCKEY: F.FOX.
COLOURS: MR. A. STEDALL.

BLERIOT'S NEW AEROPLANE

How to Keep Fit

No 19

For Chewing
and Smoking

MAYO'S
CUT PLUG
IS ALWAYS GOOD

P.H.Mayo & Brother
INCOR.

RICHMOND
VA.

ADMIRAL
FRENCH NAVY

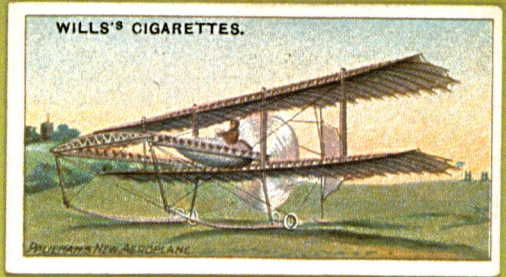

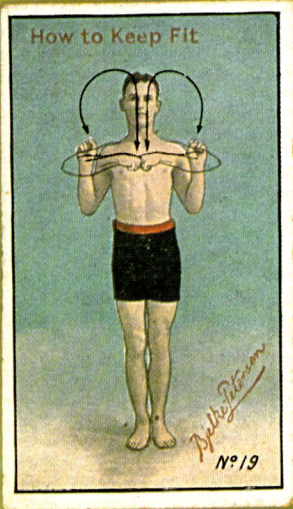

Countryman—"Tinfinder
Won Melbourne Cup 1882
Mr. J. E. Saville   Jockey, Hutchins
Age—5   Weight—7 13   Time—3.40

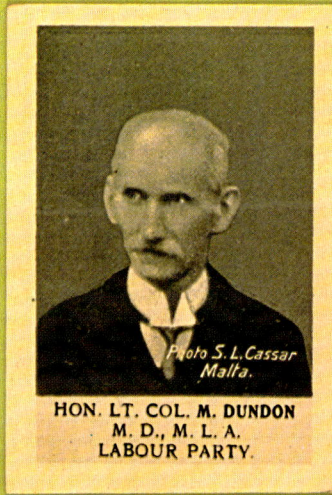

THE ASSYRIAN

H·M·S·HINDUSTAN

H.M.S. HINDUSTAN
Battleship (Pre-Dreadnought)
16,350 tons

SCOUT BADGES

BOY
SCOUTS

BOY
SCOUTS

HEALTHYMAN

Photo S. L. Cassar
Malta.

HON. LT. COL. M. DUNDON
M. D., M. L. A.
LABOUR PARTY.

AMERICAN
ADMIRAL

FOR BRAVERY · VIR DAPPERHEID

ALMANACH
voortjaar
1796

Gedrukt by, I. C. RITTER.
Aan.CAAP de.GOEDEHOOP

172

FRENCH NOVELTIES

25 DIFFERENT CARDS.

Packed in

Honest LONG CUT.

FOR

SMOKING AND CHEWING

Manufactured by

W. Duke Sons & Co.

THE AMERICAN TOBACCO CO.

SUCCESSOR

NEW YORK, U.S.A.

173

❋ 25 ILLUSTRATED SONGS. ❋

COMIN' THRO' THE RYE.

Gin a body meet a body comin' thro' the rye,
Gin a body kiss a body need a body cry?
Ilka lassie has her laddie; nane they say ha'e I,
Yet a' the lads they smile at me when comin' thro'
    the rye.

Gin a body meet a body comin' frae the town,
Gin a body meet a body need a body frown?
Ilka lassie has her laddie; nane they say ha'e I,
Yet a' the lads they smile at me when comin' thro'
    the rye.

Amang the train there is a swain I dearly love
    mysel';
But what's his name or where's his hame I dinna
    choose to tell.
Ilka lassie has her laddie; nane they say ha'e I,
Yet a' the lads they smile at me when comin' thro'
    the rye.

HONEST LONG CUT

◉ SMOKING & CHEWING TOBACCO ◉

Manufactured by

W. DUKE SONS & CO.

BRANCH OF

The American Tobacco Co. NEW YORK.

GEO. S. HARRIS & SONS, LITH. PHILA.

174

FOREIGN BIRDS

A SERIES OF 50

6

Lazuli Bunting.

(*Passerina amœna*).

The Lazuli Bunting or Finch is about 5 ½ inches in total length, and is a native of Southern Canada and the United States, migrating south and spending the winter in Mexico. The brilliant colouring of the male bird suggests a tropical setting, while the female wears a more homely dress devoid of the bright blue of her mate. The Lazuli Bunting has a pleasing song, and is a rather shy bird, concealing itself in the shelter of shrubs and thickets.

175

EAGLE BIRD

10 CIGARETTES LARGE SIZE.

CIGARETTES

MANUFACTURED BY
BRITISH AMERICAN TOBACCO CO. LTD.
IN UNITED STATES OF AMERICA.

176

THIS SURFACE IS ADHESIVE.

CORONATION SERIES

CEREMONIAL DRESS

50 SUBJECTS

26

THE MOST DISTINGUISHED ORDER OF ST. MICHAEL AND ST. GEORGE (G.C.M.G.)

This Order was originally established in 1818 to commemorate the placing of the Ionian Islands under British protection. The Order has since been enlarged, and is now conferred on persons who render valuable services in or in relation to the Oversea Dominions, or in connection with foreign affairs. It is divided into three classes: Knights Grand Cross, Knights Commanders, and Companions. Certain members of the Order are summoned to represent it at the Coronation Ceremony. The Mantle illustrated will be worn by Knights Grand Cross who are not Peers.

JOHN PLAYER & SONS

177

THIS SURFACE IS ADHESIVE.

NATIONAL FLAGS AND ARMS

A SERIES OF 50

26

JAPAN

Known as the "Land of the Rising Sun," it is not surprising to find that a conventional form of sun forms Japan's national flag and ensign. The national flag shows the red disc of the sun without any rays at all, while all of the Service flags display the red ball of the sun with varying numbers of rays. The emblem is the Chrysanthemum, showing 16 petals as illustrated. This is the State *Mon* of the Emperor, the *Kiku-no-hana-no-mon*. The *mon* of the Japanese nobility are their family devices or tokens, and correspond to the Western Coats of Arms or heraldic badges.

JOHN PLAYER & SONS

178

CAMERON & CAMERON,

Richmond, Virginia.
U.S.A.,

Celebrated Cigarettes
Superior to all,

RECEIVING
the only Award at the
World's
Columbian Exposition,
Chicago, 1893.

179

CINEMA CELEBRITIES (C)

This is one of a series of pictures now being packed with these cigarettes.

(24)

GARY COOPER

FAMOUS FILM STAR

180

JERSEY

PAST AND PRESENT

THIRD SERIES

S.S. "ISLE OF JERSEY"

(From the original painting by J. D. Attwood)

Built by Wm. Denny Bros. Dumbarton, in 1930 to carry 800 first class and 600 second class passengers. Tonnage 2,143. Length 306 ft. Beam 42 ft. Twin Screw turbine. Speed 19¼ knots. Her sister ship was the "Isle of Guernsey" followed later by the "Isle of Sark." During the 1939/45 War she served as a hospital ship, being based at Scapa Flow. She returned to the Southampton/Channel Islands service after the War until the first months of 1960 when she was sold for service in the Mediterranean after alterations on the Tyne, and renamed the "Libda."

No. 19

This is one of a series of 24 landscape views, modern and historical, being packed with these high grade cigarettes.

Comin' thro' the Rye.

PLAYER'S CIGARETTES

JAPAN

PLAYER'S CIGARETTES

THE ORDER OF ST. MICHAEL
AND ST. GEORGE

นางมณโฑ

LAZULI BUNTING

S.S. "ISLE OF JERSEY"

GARY COOPER

Fireman

November

MAI BACON

Bonne Nuit Bay- Jersey

WILLS'S CIGARETTES

THE "QUEEN MARY"

J. DAVIS

WILL'S CIGARETTES.
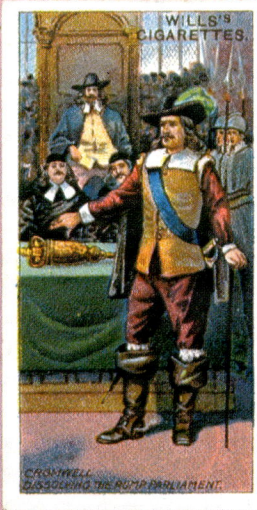
CROMWELL DISSOLVING THE RUMP PARLIAMENT.

PLAYER'S CIGARETTES
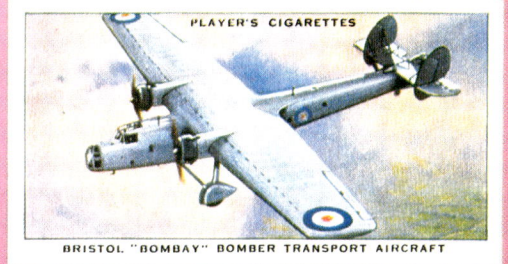
BRISTOL "BOMBAY" BOMBER TRANSPORT AIRCRAFT

PLAYER'S CIGARETTES

GREY GURNARD

PLAYER'S CIGARETTES

GOLD COAST REGIMENT

PLAYER'S CIGARETTES

W. R. HAMMOND

WILLS'S CIGARETTES

COVERING A ROOF WITH BITUMEN FELT

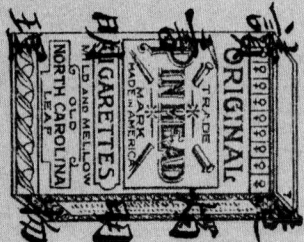

195

FLEURS DE CULTURE

UNE SERIE DE 25

6.
LE NARCISSE

Ce nom englobe générale-
ment plusieurs variétés y com-
pris le narcisse des bois,
quoiqu'il soit plus spécialement
associé à la variété de petites
fleurs à deux tons. La variété
appelée primevère donne
plusieurs fleurs sur une même
tige et fleurit au début de la
saison. La terre grasse con-
vient mieux à leur culture, mais
les plantes sont suffisamment
robustes pour pousser dans
n'importe quel terrain.

L'atout imbattable!

DOMINO
FILTER

196

No 47
ARMS OF THE BRITISH EMPIRE

WILLS'S CIGARETTES

Straits Settlements.

This device has never
been officially assigned,
but is in general use as
the arms of the Straits
Settlements. The colony
consists of Singapore,
Penang and Malacca,
all three settlements being
situated on the Straits
of Malacca. The Cocos
Islands were added in 1886,
and Christmas Island was
annexed in 1900.

W.D. & H.O. WILLS,
BRISTOL & LONDON.

197

PICTURES OF THE EAST

A SERIES OF 48
REAL STEREOSCOPIC
PHOTOGRAPHS.

No 15

Threshing.

Whilst magnificent work has been
and is being done in Egypt to help
the agriculture, it has naturally been
done on modern and up-to-date lines,
and the phenomenon occurs. It is, therefore,
with some surprise that one notices
still in use methods that are centuries
old and primitive beyond belief. The
photograph is a good illustration. It
will be seen that the method of
threshing is simply to toss the grain
into the air in order that the chaff
may blow away.

198

N.Z. BUTTERFLIES, MOTHS & BEETLES.

A SERIES OF 50
43

Long-snouted Plant
Bug.
Thanatodictya
tillyardi.

This is the most strik-
ing of the very few plant
bugs found in New Zea-
land. It is found only
in the South Island and
is rather rare.

(Four times life size.)

W.D. & H.O. WILLS
BRISTOL & LONDON

199

PETER PAN
Mild and Mellow

NATIVE BEAR

A harmless marsupial, very
tenacious of life. A splendid
tree climber. Sometimes
called Monkey-Bear. Its
solitary young one clings to
its back.—Australian.

CIGARETTES
10 with Holders 10

O. & Co.

200

MODERN BEAUTIES
7

THIS IS ONE OF
A SERIES OF 36
PHOTOGRAPHS
NOW BEING
PACKED WITH
THESE
CIGARETTES

SECOND SERIES

201

A SERIES OF 25
ARMY LIFE.
No. 16

Unpacking Waggons.

Most of the military
waggons can be
packed with the same
careful economy of
space as the Army
Service Corps waggon
illustrated. In competitions in which prizes are
offered to those units
which can "unpack" their
"goods" and pack up in
the quickest time, these
sixty seconds, and still it is dis-
tinctly a feat of ingenuity and
ready for shipment.

202

KEEP FIT
A SERIES OF 50
7

Exercises for Women

By the Hon. Coach to the British
Women's Olympic Team, 1936

BODY ROCKING
An exercise for developing the
back, and also strengthening the
thigh muscles. Lie face down-
wards and try to lift the legs and
shoulders from the ground, keeping the arms straight (A). Lower
the face to the ground, keeping
the legs raised, without lifting
the arms (B). Try to make a
"rocker" of the body, performing
the movement at a fast pace, as a
push-up rocker at a time, with
lower the legs and at the same
time raise the trunk and at the same
still trying to keep the arms up to
the sides and still making the
"rocking" movement (C). This
is not an easy exercise and should
only be attempted by the fittest.
At first it should be performed
three or four times only.

203

WONDERS OF THE WORLD.

14
Shway Dagon Pagoda,
Rangoon.

On a hillside one hundred and sixty-
six feet above Rangoon stands the
bewildering assemblage of shrines,
pagodas, and colossal animals which
constitute this monument of Burmese
Buddhism, the Shway Dagon. The
central Pagoda is 368 feet high (taller
than St. Paul's), and is of solid brick
overlaid with pure gold. The glitter-
ing cone is surmounted by a vane
encrusted with about 4,600 diamonds,
rubies, &c.

THIS IS ONE OF A SERIES
OF 25 PICTURES
NOW BEING PACKED
WITH THESE CIGARETTES

204

PICTURESQUE PEOPLE OF THE EMPIRE
A SERIES OF 25

11
Canadian Trapper.

The pursuit of fur-bearing
animals in the vast solitudes of
the frozen north and west has
not only been a valuable source
of revenue, but has played an
important part in the development of Canada since the days
of the old Hudson's Bay Company, which was incorporated
by Charles II as long ago as
1670. The most important pelts
or skins taken at the present
day are fox, muskrat, beaver,
mink, marten, coyote and otter.
In the year 1923-4 the total
value of the pelts taken ex-
ceeded three million sterling.

W.D. & H.O. WILLS
BRISTOL & LONDON

205

PAST & PRESENT
A SERIES OF 25

20
The Organ.

EARLY FORM OF ORGAN.—The pipes
of early organs at first sounded all together, those not required being silen-
ced by means of the fingers or hands.
Slides or tongues of wood were then
placed beneath the pipes to control the
admission of the wind, whence there
shown on the right of the wind-chest,
and may be regarded to represent the
key-board of the organ of to-day.

MODERN ORGAN.—The picture shows
part of one of the largest electric organs in the world with some 18,000
pipes and 232 stops. It really comprises eight organs: great, choir, swell,
solo, echo, chorus, ethereal, and pedal,
besides a piano, chimes, gongs, and
harp.

W.D. & H.O. WILLS
BRISTOL & LONDON

206

· MELBOURNE CUP WINNERS ·

BRISEIS, 1876.
TIM WHIFFLER—MUSIDORA.

B F, 3 years   Weight, 6.4.   Time, 3.36.

Owner: Trainer: Jockey:
J. Wilson, sen.   J. Wilson.   P. St. Albans.

2nd, Sybil, 6.0; 3rd, Timothy, 7.0.

Starters, 33.   Starting price, 7 to 1.

Colors Black jacket, white cap.

207

A. G. COUSIS & Co.
CAIRO-MALTA.

Speciality of the Firm
»DUBEC« BRAND

Manufacturers also of
Virginia Cigarettes blended
from purest tobacco
warranted free from
chemical substances.

No. 34

208

NATURAL AND MAN MADE WONDERS OF THE WORLD
49

The Mariposa Big Tree

The Mariposa Big Tree is in the
Yosemite National Park, California.
This Park was given by Congress to
the State of California in 1864, and it
is famous for the gigantic and beautiful redwood trees which exist in no
other part of the world. Some of
these giants have names, and one of
them, the Wawona in Mariposa Wood,
has had a gateway made through it
which allows vehicles to pass.

SERIES OF 50

WILL'S CIGARETTES.

STRAITS SETTLEMENTS.

ARMS OF THE BRITISH EMPIRE.

CURTISS "YP-40"

DAILY MAIL

JUNE KNIGHT

NATIVE BEAR.

LONG-SNOUTED PLANT BUG

CANADIAN TRAPPER.

SHWAY DAGON PAGODA, RANGOON.

UNHOOKING WAGGON.

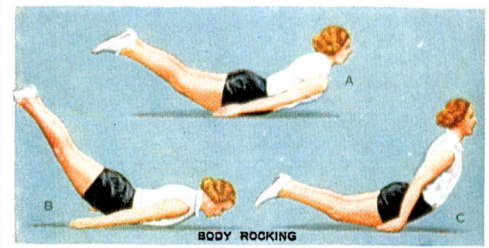

BODY ROCKING

Virgmio Talli

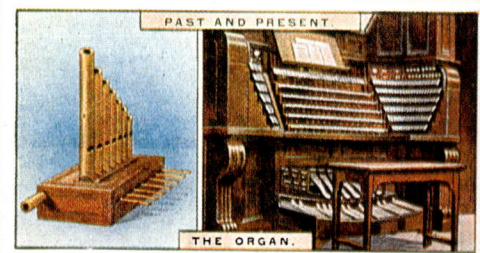

PAST AND PRESENT.

THE ORGAN.

BRISEIS

PART THREE

AFRICAN CIGARETTE CO. LTD. Egypt

Illus. No.	Size	Number in set		Price per card	Complete set
		50	Actresses ALWICS (1905–08)	£4.00	—
	L	25	Auction Bridge (1925–30)	£2.50	—

AFRICAN TOBACCO MANUFACTURERS, South Africa

A. Card Issues

Illus. No.	Size	Number in set		Price per card	Complete set
	L	18	All Blacks South African Tour (1928)	—	—
164		60	Animals (1920–25):—		
			A. Cut Outs	£2.00	—
			B. Not Cut Out	£1.25	—
		25	The Arcadia Fair (1924)	£4.00	—
	MP	48	British Aircraft (1932)	£2.00	—
		50	Chinese Transport (1930)	£2.50	—
	MP	48	Cinema Artistes (1930)	80p	—
		50	Cinema Stars "OMBI" Officers Mess Issue 1st Series (1921)	60p	—
		50	Cinema Stars "OMBI" Officers Mess Issue 2nd Series (1921)	75p	—
	M	50	Famous & Beautiful Women (1938)	90p	—
	L	50	Famous & Beautiful Women (1938)	70p	—
		33	Houses of Parliament (1920–25)	£4.00	—
		58	Miniatures (1925–30)	£3.50	—
	MP	48	National Costume (1930)	£1.00	—
	K	53	Playing Cards MP–SA Virginia Cigarettes (1930–35)	50p	—
	K	53	Playing Cards OK Cigarettes (1930–35)	50p	—
	K	53	Playing Cards Scots Cigarettes (1930–35)	50p	—
	MP	48	Popular Dogs (1930)	£1.00	—
39	M	100	Postage Stamps Rarest Varieties (1929)	60p	£60.00
	M	80	Prominent NZ & Australian Rugby Players & Springbok 1937 Touring Team (1937)	60p	—
	L	80	Prominent NZ & Australian Rugby Players & Springbok 1937 Touring Team (1937)	50p	—
		25	The Racecourse (1924)	£3.50	—
	M	132	S. African Members of the Legislative Assembly (1921)	—	—
166	M	100	The World of Sport (1938)	40p	—
	L	100	The World of Sport (1938)	40p	—

B. Silk Issues

Illus. No.	Size	Number in set		Price per card	Complete set
	M	30	Some Beautiful Roses (1920–25)	£4.00	—
	M	25	Types of British Birds (1920–25)	£4.00	—
	M	20	Types of British Butterflies (1920–25)	£4.00	—
	M	25	Types of Railway Engines (1920–25)	£7.00	—
	M	25	Types of Sea Shells (1920–25)	£5.00	—

ALLEN & GINTER, U.S.A.

All series issued 1885–95

Illus. No.	Size	Number in set		Price per card	Complete set
		?	Actors & Actresses (Sepia Photographic)	£1.00	—
		?	Actresses & Beauties (Coloured)	£4.00	—
		50	American Editors	£6.00	—
	L	50	American Editors	£7.50	—
		50	Arms of All Nations	£6.00	—
43		50	Birds of America	£3.50	£175.00
	L	50	Birds of America	£7.50	—
		50	Birds of the Tropics	£4.00	£200.00
	L	50	Birds of the Tropics	£7.50	—
		50	Celebrated American Indian Chiefs	£5.00	£250.00
		50	City Flags	£4.00	—
		50	Fans of the Period	£6.00	—
		50	Fish from American Waters	£4.00	—
	L	50	Fish from American Waters	£7.50	—
		50	Flags of All Nations (Series Title Curved)	£3.00	£150.00
		48	Flags of All Nations (Series Title in Straight Line)	£3.00	£150.00
		50	Flags of All Nations 2nd Series	£3.00	£150.00
		47	Flags of the States & Territories	£3.50	—
		50	Fruits	£5.00	£250.00
		50	Game Birds	£3.00	£150.00
	L	50	Game Birds	£7.50	—
		50	General Government & State Capitol Buildings	£4.50	—
		50	Great Generals	£8.00	—
		50	Natives in Costume	£8.00	—
		50	Naval Flags	£4.00	—
		50	Parasol Drill	£5.00	£250.00
		50	Pirates of the Spanish Main	£6.00	—
143		50	Prize and Game Chickens	£3.00	£150.00
		50	Quadrupeds	£4.00	—
	L	50	Quadrupeds	£7.50	—
		50	Racing Colors of the World:—		
			a) Front with White Frame	£4.00	—
			b) Front without White Frame	£6.00	—
		50	Song Birds of the World	£4.00	—
	L	50	Song Birds of the World	£7.50	—
		50	Types of All Nations	£5.00	£250.00
34		50	Wild Animals of the World	£4.00	£200.00
		50	The Worlds Beauties 1st Series	£5.00	£250.00
		50	The Worlds Beauties 2nd Series	£5.00	—
		50	The World's Champions 1st Series	£3.50	£175.00
		50	The World's Champions 2nd Series	£5.00	—
	L	50	The World's Champions 2nd Series	£7.50	—
		50	The Worlds Decorations	£5.00	£250.00

ALLEN & GINTER, U.S.A. *(continued)*

Illus. No.	Size	Number in set		Price per card	Complete set
	L	50	The Worlds Decorations	£7.50	—
		50	Worlds Dudes	£5.00	—
		50	The Worlds Racers	£6.00	—
33		50	Worlds Smokers	£5.00	—
		50	World's Sovereigns	£8.00	—

ALLEN TOBACCO CO., U.S.A. ⸻

	L	?	Views and Art Studies (1910–15)	£2.00	—

THE AMERICAN CIGARETTE CO., LTD., China ⸻

		25	Beauties Group 1 (1885–95)	£12.00	—
		?15	Beauties Group 2 (1885–95)	£15.00	—
		50	Flowers (1885–95)	£6.00	—

THE AMERICAN TOBACCO COMPANY, U.S.A. ⸻

Issues 1890–1900
A. Typeset Back in Black

		28	Beauties Domino Girls......................................	£8.00	—
		25	Beauties Group 1 RB18/4	£2.50	—
		?1	Beauties Group 2 RB18/20	—	—
		25	Beauties Group 3 RB18/25	£2.50	—
		27	Beauties Group 3 RB18/26	£3.00	£80.00
		25	Beauties Group 3 RB18/27	£3.00	—
		25	Beauties Group 3 RB18/29	—	—
			Beauties Group 4 RB18/36: —		
		50	a) Coloured	£2.00	£100.00
		?50	b) Sepia	£15.00	—
		52	Beauties P.C. Inset......................................	£3.00	£150.00
		25	Beauties – Star Girls	£7.00	—
		25	Dancers	£4.00	—
		50	Dancing Women	£6.00	—
		50	Fancy Bathers	£4.50	—
		36	Japanese Girls..	—	—
		25	Military Uniforms RB18/101	£4.00	—
44		25	Military Uniforms RB18/102	£4.00	—
		27	Military Uniforms RB18/103	£3.00	£80.00
		50	Musical Instruments....................................	£6.00	—
		50	National Flag & Arms	£4.00	—
		25	National Flag & Flowers – Girls –	£7.50	—
		50	Savage Chiefs & Rulers	£5.00	—

B. Net Design Back in Green

		25	Beauties – black background RB18/62	£4.00	—
		25	Beauties – Curtain Background RB18/65	£3.00	£75.00
		25	Beauties Flower Girls RB18/67	£4.00	—
		25	Beauties Group 1 RB18/1	£2.00	£50.00
		27	Beauties Group 1 RB18/2	£2.50	—
		25	Beauties Group 1 RB18/3	£2.00	—
		24	Beauties Group 1 RB18/4	£3.00	—
		25	Beauties Group 1 RB18/5	£2.50	—
		25	Beauties Group 1 RB18/6	£2.00	£50.00
		50	Beauties Group 1 RB18/10	£2.00	—
		25	Beauties Group 2 RB18/16	£2.50	—
		25	Beauties Group 2 RB18/17	£2.50	—
		?24	Beauties Group 2 RB18/18	£2.50	—
		25	Beauties Group 2 RB18/19	£2.50	—
		25	Beauties Group 2 RB18/20	£2.50	—
		25	Beauties Group 2 RB18/21	£4.00	—
		36	Beauties Group 2 RB18/22	£5.00	—
		25	Beauties Group 3 RB18/25	£2.50	—
		?10	Beauties Group 3 RB18/28	—	—
		25	Beauties Group 3 RB18/30	£3.00	—
		25	Beauties Group 3 RB18/31	£7.50	—
		25	Beauties Group 3 RB18/32	£3.50	—
		50	Beauties Marine & Universe Girls	£5.00	—
		25	Beauties Palette Girls	£5.00	—
		25	Beauties Star Girls.....................................	£7.50	—
		25	Beauties – stippled background RB18/78..................	£4.00	—
		20	Beauties – thick border RB18/79........................	—	—
41		52	Beauties with Playing Card inset Set 1 RB18/85	£3.00	—
		52	Beauties with Playing Card inset Set 2 RB18/86	£3.00	£150.00
		25	Boer War Series II – Series A: —		
			a) numbered....................................	£2.00	£50.00
			b) unnumbered	£2.00	—
			c) unnumbered and untitled "series A"............	£4.00	—
		22	Boer War Series II – Series B	£2.50	£55.00
		25	Chinese Girls...	—	—
		25	Fish from American Waters	£3.00	—
		25	International Code of Signals	£4.00	—
		27	Military Uniforms numbered.............................	£3.00	—
		25	Military Uniforms unnumbered	£4.00	—
		50	National Flags & Arms	—	—
170		25	Old & Ancient Ships 1st Series..........................	£2.00	£50.00
		25	Old & Ancient Ships 2nd Series.........................	£4.00	£100.00

Illus. No.	Size	Number in set		Price per card	Complete set
		25	Star Series – Beauties	£6.00	—
C. Net Design Back in Blue					
			Actresses:—		
	P	?300	A. Large Letter Back.................................	£1.75	—
	P	?300	B. Small Letter Back.................................	£3.00	—
		25	Beauties Blue Frameline:—		
			A. Matt	—	—
			B. Varnished	—	—
		28	Beauties – Domino Girls	£8.00	—
		28	Beauties Group 1 Dull Backgrounds......................	£4.00	—
		23	Beauties Group 1 Vivid Coloured backgrounds Set 1	£4.00	—
		25	Beauties Group 1 Vivid Coloured backgrounds Set 2	£4.00	—
		25	Beauties:—		
			A. Front in black and white	—	—
			B. Front in mauve	£4.00	—
		24	Beauties – Orange framelines...........................	—	—
			Beauties – Playing cards:—		
		52	A. Inscribed 52 subjects	£3.00	—
		53	B. Inscribed 53 subjects	£3.00	—
		32	Celebrities..	£2.50	—
		25	Comic Scenes..	£4.00	—
	P	?149	Views	£1.50	—
D. "Old Gold" Back					
		25	Beauties Group 1 RB18/1	£2.00	—
		27	Beauties Group 1 RB18/2	£1.50	—
		25	Beauties Group 1 RB18/3	£1.50	—
		24	Beauties Group 1 RB18/4	£2.00	—
		25	Beauties Group 1 RB18/5	£2.00	—
		25	Beauties Group 1 RB18/6	£2.00	—
		?47	Beauties Group 2 RB18/16,17,18	£2.00	—
		25	Beauties Group 2 RB18/22	£2.00	—
		25	Beauties Group 3 RB18/25	£2.00	£50.00
		27	Beauties Group 3 RB18/26	£2.00	£55.00
		25	Beauties Group 3 RB18/27	£1.50	—
		25	Beauties Group 3 RB18/28	£2.00	—
		25	Beauties Group 3 RB18/30	£2.00	—
169		25	Flowers Inset on Beauties	£3.00	£75.00
		25	International Code of Signals:—		
			A. With Series Title	£3.00	£75.00
			B. Without Series Title..............................	£3.00	£75.00
E. Labels Back					
		35	Beauties Group 1 RB18/2–3	£2.00	—
		25	Beauties Group 2 1st Set RB18/15	£2.00	—
		25	Beauties Group 2 2nd Set RB18/16	£2.00	—
			Beauties Group 3 RB18/25–26:—		
		27	A. Old Gold Label	£2.00	—
		26	B. Brands Label	£2.00	—
F. Other Backs with Name of Firm					
	P	100	Actresses RB18/91....................................	£2.00	—
		44	Australian Parliament	£3.00	£135.00
		25	Battle Scenes	£4.00	—
		1	Columbian & Other Postage Stamps.....................	—	£6.00
		50	Congress of Beauty – Worlds Fair	£8.00	—
		50	Fish from American Waters	£3.00	—
		50	Flags of All Nations	—	—
		25	Flower Inset on Beauties	£3.00	£75.00
		25	International Code of Signals	£3.00	£75.00
		25	Songs A:—		
			A. Thicker board size 70 × 39 mm......................	£4.00	—
			B. Thinner board size 67 × 39 mm	£3.00	£75.00
		25	Songs B:—		
			A. Size 70 × 39 mm..................................	£3.00	£75.00
			B. Size 67 × 39 mm..................................	£4.00	—
		25	Songs C 1st Series....................................	£2.50	£62.50
		25	Songs C 2nd Series...................................	£3.50	—
		25	Songs D	£3.00	£75.00
46		25	Songs E	£3.50	—
		25	Songs F	£4.00	—
		25	Songs G..	£4.00	£100.00
		25	Songs H	£5.00	—
		25	Songs I	£6.00	—
Issues 1900–1940					
	L	50	Actors	80p	—
		80	Actress Series..	—	—
	L	50	Actresses...	—	—
	L	80	Animals:—		
			A. Descriptive back.................................	75p	—
			B. Non Descriptive back	75p	—
	L	25	Arctic Scenes	£1.00	—
	M	15	Art Gallery Pictures	—	—
	M	50	Art Reproductions....................................	—	—
		21	Art Series	—	—
		18	Ask Dad	—	—
	L	50	Assorted Standard Bearers of Different Countries	—	—
		25	Auto-drivers	—	—

Illus. No.	Size	Number in set		Price per card	Complete set
	M	50	Automobile Series	—	—
	L	50	Baseball Folder Series (T201)	£3.00	—
	M	121	Baseball Series (T204)	—	—
146		208	Baseball Series (T205)	£4.00	—
145		522	Baseball Series (T206)	£3.00	—
		200	Baseball Series (T207)	£6.00	—
		565	Baseball Series (T210)	—	—
		75	Baseball Series (T211)	—	—
		426	Baseball Series (T212)	—	—
		180	Baseball Series (T213)	—	—
		90	Baseball Series (T214)	—	—
		100	Baseball Series (T215)	—	—
	L	76	Baseball Triple Folders (T202)	£10.00	—
		100	Bird Series:—		
			A. With White Borders	60p	—
			B. With Gold Borders	60p	—
		30	Bird Series with Fancy Gold Frame	75p	—
	M	360	Birthday Horoscopes	£1.00	—
	M	24	British Buildings "Tareyton" issue	80p	—
	M	42	British Sovereigns "Tareyton" issue	80p	—
	M	50	Butterfly Series	—	—
	L	153	Champion Athlete & Prize Fighter Series (Size 73 × 64 mm)	50p	—
	L	50	Champion Athlete & Prize Fighter Series (Size 83 × 63 mm)	£1.00	—
	L	50	Champion Pugilists	£2.00	—
	EL	100	Champion Women Swimmers	£2.50	—
	M	150	College series	50p	—
	M	50	Costumes & Scenery for All Countries of the World	£1.25	—
142	L	49	Cowboy Series	£1.00	—
	M	38	Cross Stitch	—	—
	M	17	Embarrassing Moments or Emotional Moments	—	—
	M	50	Emblem Series	£1.00	—
	L	100	Fable Series	75p	—
	LP	53	Famous Baseball Players, American Athletic Champions & Photoplay Stars	—	—
		50	Fish Series inscribed "1 to 50"	60p	—
		100	Fish Series inscribed "1 to 100"	60p	—
		200	Flags of All Nations	50p	—
	M	100	Flags of All Nations	—	—
		50	Foreign Stamp Series	—	—
	L	505	Fortune Series	75p	—
	M	79	Henry "Tareyton" issue	60p	—
	L	50	Heroes of History	£1.00	—
	M	50	Historic Homes	60p	—
	L	25	Historical Events Series	£1.00	—
	M	25	Hudson – Fulton Series	—	—
160	L	50	Indian Life in the 60's	£1.00	—
	L	221	Jig Saw Puzzle Pictures	—	—
	L	50	Light House Series	£1.00	—
	L	50	Men of History	£1.00	—
		100	Military Series White borders	£2.00	—
		50	Military Series Gilt borders	£3.00	—
		50	Military Series "Recruit" issue:—		
			A. Uncut Cards	£2.00	—
			B. Die-Cut Cards	£2.00	—
		50	Movie Stars	—	—
	L	100	Movie Stars	—	—
		15	Moving Picture Stars	—	—
	EL	50	Murad Post Card Series	—	—
		100	Mutt & Jeff Series (Black & White)	£1.50	—
		100	Mutt & Jeff Series (Coloured)	£2.00	—
	EL	16	National League & American League Teams	—	—
		50	Pugilistic Subjects	—	—
	EL	18	Puzzle Picture Cards	—	—
	M	200	Riddle Series	60p	—
	EL	60	Royal Bengal Souvenir Cards	—	—
	M	150	Seals of the United States & Coats of Arms	50p	—
	L	25	Series of Champions	—	—
	L	50	Sights & Scenes of the World	£1.00	—
	L	50	Silhouettes	—	—
	L	25	Song Bird Series	—	—
		38	Sports Champions	—	—
		45	Stage Stars	—	—
		25	State Girl Series	—	—
	L	50	Theatres Old & New Series	£1.25	—
	M	50	Toast Series	—	—
	M	550	Toast Series	—	—
	L	25	Toasts	—	—
		50	Types of Nations:—		
			A. Without Series Title	£1.00	—
			B. With Series Title	£1.00	—
			C. Anonymous Back	£1.00	—
	L	25	Up to date baseball Comics	—	—
	L	25	Up to date Comics	—	—
	P	340	World Scenes & Portraits	—	—
		250	World War I Scenes	75p	—
	L	50	Worlds Champion Athletes	—	—
	L	25	The Worlds Greatest Explorers	80p	—

THE AMERICAN TOBACCO CO. OF NEW SOUTH WALES LTD., Australia

Illus. No.	Size	Number in set		Price per card	Complete set
		25	Beauties Group 1 RB18/8 (1895–1905)......................	£4.00	—
		25	Beauties Group 2 (1895–1905).............................	£4.00	—

THE AMERICAN TOBACCO CO. OF VICTORIA LTD., Australia

		?87	Beauties Group 2 (1895–1905)..............................	£5.00	—

ATLAM CIGARETTE FACTORY, Malta

	M	65	Beauties Back in Blue (1920–30)...........................	90p	—
		150	Beauties Back in Brown (1920–30)..........................	—	—
167	M	519	Celebrities (1920–30).....................................	50p	—
	L	50	Views of Malta (1920–30).................................	—	—
	M	128	Views of the World	90p	—

BANNER TOBACCO CO., U.S.A.

	L	25	Girls (1885–95)...	£7.50	—

THOMAS BEAR & SONS LTD.

		50	Aeroplanes (1926)	£1.25	—
		50	Cinema Artistes Set 2 (1928–33)	—	—
		50	Cinema Artistes Set 4 (1928–33)	—	—
		50	Cinema Stars Coloured (1930).............................	80p	£40.00
52		50	Do You Know (1923).....................................	50p	£25.00
		270	Javanese Series 1 Blue Background (1925–40)	50p	—
		100	Javanese Series 4 Yellow Background (1925–40).............	—	—
		50	Stage & Film Stars (1926)	£1.00	—

AUG BECK & CO. U.S.A.

		29	Picture Cards (1885–95)..................................	£10.00	—

J. & F. BELL LTD., Denmark

		60	Rigvaabner (1920–30).....................................	£8.00	—
		60	Women of Nations (1924).................................	£10.00	—

BENSON & HEDGES (CANADA) LTD.

42		48	Ancient & Modern Fire Fighting Equipment (1947)	80p	£40.00

BRITISH AMERICAN TOBACCO CO. LTD.

A With Makers Name Net Design in Green

		25	Beauties Art Series RB18/61................................	£6.00	—
		25	Beauties – Black Background RB18/62	£4.00	—
		25	Beauties – Blossom Girls RB18/63..........................	£10.00	—
		25	Beauties – Flower Girls RB18/67	£4.00	—
47		25	Beauties – Fruit Girls RB18/68	£5.00	—
		25	Beauties – Girls in Costumes RB18/69	£3.50	—
		20	Beauties Group 1 RB18/9	£3.50	—
		25	Beauties – Lantern Girls RB18/70	£3.50	£87.50
		50	Beauties – Marine & Universe Girls RB18/71	£4.00	—
		25	Beauties – Palette Girls RB18/74:—		
			A. Plain Border to Front	£3.00	—
			B. Red Border to Front	£5.00	—
		24	Beauties – Smoke Girls RB18/75	—	—
		25	Beauties – Star Girls RB18/76	£5.00	—
27		25	Beauties – Stippled Background RB18/78....................	£3.50	£87.50
		25	Beauties – Water Girls RB18/80	£4.00	£100.00
		50	Buildings RB18/131	£3.00	—
		25	Chinese Girls "A" RB18/111...............................	£4.00	—
		25	Chinese Girls "B" RB18/112:—		
			A. Background Plain...................................	£3.00	—
			B. Background with Chinese Letters.....................	£3.00	£75.00
		25	Chinese Girls "C" RB18/113..............................	£3.00	£75.00
		25	Chinese Girls "D" RB18/114..............................	£3.00	£75.00
		25	Chinese Girls "E" RB18/115..............................	£3.00	—
		25	Chinese Girls "F" Set 1 RB18/116.........................	£3.00	—
		25	Chinese Girls "F" Set 2 RB18/116:—		
			A. Yellow Border......................................	£3.00	—
			B. Gold Border.......................................	—	—
		50	Chinese Girls "F" Set 3:—		
			A. Plain Background...................................	£3.00	£150.00
			B. Chinese Characters Background.......................	£5.00	—
		40	Chinese Trades	£3.00	—

BRITISH AMERICAN TOBACCO CO. LTD. *(continued)*

Illus. No.	Size	Number in set		Price per card	Complete set
B	*With Makers Name Net Design in Blue*				
		25	Beauties – Numbered	—	—
		53	Beauties – Playing Cards	£3.00	—
C	*With Makers Name Other Backs*				
	MP	50	Beauties (1925)	50p	£25.00
	MP	40	Beauties (1926)	60p	—
	M	50	Birds, Beast & Fishes (1925)	60p	£30.00
		50	Danish Athletes (1905)	—	—
		28	Dominoes (1905)	£1.50	—
		48	Fairy Tales (1926)	—	—
		48	A Famous Picture – The Toast (1925–36)	—	—
		25	New York Views (1905–10)	—	—
		53	Playing Cards (1905)	£3.00	—
163	M	50	Wild Animals (1930–35)	50p	—
D	*Series with Brand Names*				
	Albert Cigarettes				
	M	50	Aeroplanes (Civil) (1935)	—	—
		50	Artistes De Cinema Nd 1–50 (1932)	£1.00	—
		50	Artistes De Cinema Nd 51–100 (1933)	£1.00	—
	M	75	Belles Vues De Belgique (1925–30)	80p	—
	M	50	Butterflies (Girls) (1926)	£2.00	—
	M	50	Cinema Stars (Brown Photogravure) (1927–29)	—	—
	M	100	Cinema Stars (Numbered, Coloured) (1927–29)	80p	—
	M	208	Cinema Stars (Unnumbered, Coloured) (1927–29)	80p	—
165	M	100	Circus Scenes (1925–35)	£1.00	—
	M	100	Famous Beauties (1916)	£1.50	—
	M	50	L'Afrique Equitoriale De L'est A L'ouest (1930–35)	£1.25	—
	M	100	La Faune Congolaise (1930–35)	80p	—
	M	50	Les Grandes Paquebots Du Monde (1924)	£2.50	—
	M	50	Merveilles Du Monde (1927)	£1.00	—
	M	50	Women of Nations (Flag Girls) (1922)	—	—
	Atlas Cigarettes				
		50	Buildings (1907)	£3.00	—
		25	Chinese Beauties (1912)	80p	£20.00
		50	Chinese Trades Set IV (1908)	60p	—
		85	Chinese Trades Set VI (1912)	70p	—
	Battle Ax Cigarettes				
	M	100	Famous Beauties (1916)	75p	—
	M	50	Women of Nations (Flag Girls) (1917)	£1.50	—
	Copain Cigarettes				
50		52	Birds of Brilliant Plumage (1927)	£1.50	—
	Domino Cigarettes				
		25	Animaux et Reptiles (1961)	7p	£1.50
		25	Corsaires et Baucaniers (1961)	7p	60p
		25	Figures Histeriques 1st Series (1961)	7p	£1.50
		25	Figures Histeriques 2nd Series (1961)	16p	£4.00
195		25	Fleurs de Culture (1961)	7p	60p
		25	Les Oiseaux et L'Art Japanais (1961)	24p	£6.00
162		25	Les Produits Du Monde (1961)	7p	50p
		50	Voitures Antiques (1961)	18p	£9.00
	Eagle Bird Cigarettes				
		50	Animals and Birds (1909)	80p	£40.00
49		50	Aviation Series (1912)	80p	—
		25	Birds of the East (1912)	70p	£17.50
		25	Chinese Famous Warriors (1911)	80p	£20.00
		25	Chinese Beauties 1st Series (1908):—		
			A. Vertical Back	80p	£20.00
			B. Horizontal Back	90p	—
		25	Chinese Beauties 2nd Series (1909):—		
			A. Front Without Framelines	£1.00	—
			B. Front With Framelines	£1.00	—
		50	Chinese Trades (1908)	60p	£30.00
		25	Cock Fighting (1911)	£1.25	£32.50
		60	Flags & Pennons (1911)	50p	£30.00
		50	Romance of the Heavens (1929)	—	—
175		50	Siamese Alphabet (1922)	50p	£25.00
		50	Siamese Dreams & Their Meanings (1923)	60p	£30.00
		50	Siamese Horoscopes (1915–18)	50p	£25.00
		50	Siamese Play-Inao (1915–18)	50p	£25.00
		50	Siamese Play-Khun Chang Khun Phaen 1st Series (1915–18)..	50p	£25.00
		50	Siamese Play-Khun Chang Khun Phaen 2nd Series (1915–18).	50p	£25.00
		36	Siamese Play-Phra Aphaiu 1st Series (1915–18)	50p	£18.00
		36	Siamese Play-Phra Aphaiu 2nd Series (1919)	50p	£18.00
		150	Siamese Play – Ramakien I (1912–14)	50p	£75.00
		50	Siamese Play – Ramakien II (1914)	50p	£25.00
		50	Siamese Uniforms (1915)	80p	£40.00
		50	Views of Siam (1928)	50p	£25.00
		50	Views of Siam (Bangkok) (1928)	50p	£25.00
		30	War Weapons (1914–15)	£1.00	£30.00
	Kong Beng Cigarettes				
37		60	Animals (cut-outs) (1912)	£3.00	—
	Mascot Cigarettes				
		100	Cinema Stars (Nd 201–300) (1931)	£1.00	—
40	M	208	Cinema Stars Unnumbered (1924)	£1.00	—
	Millbank Cigarettes				
		60	Animals (Cut-Outs):—		
			A. "1516" at base of back (1922)	80p	—

Illus. No.	Size	Number in set		Price per card	Complete set
			B. "3971" at base of back (1923)........................	50p	£30.00
Nassa Cigarettes					
	M	50	Birds, Beasts & Fishes (1924).............................	£3.00	—
Pedro Cigarettes (see also Imperial Tobacco Co. of India)					
		50	Actors & Actresses (1905–08)............................	—	—
		37	Nautch Girls Red Border (1905–07)	70p	—
Pinhead Cigarettes					
		50	Chinese Modern Beauties (1912)...........................	70p	—
		33	Chinese Heroes Set 1 (1912).............................	70p	—
		50	Chinese Heroes Set 2 (1913–14)..........................	80p	—
187		50	Chinese Trades Set III (1908)............................	50p	£25.00
		50	Chinese Trades Set IV (1909)............................	50p	£25.00
		50	Chinese Trades Set V (1910).............................	50p	£25.00
		50	Types of the British Army (1909)	£1.00	—
Railway Cigarettes (see also Imperial Tobacco Co. of India)					
		37	Nautch Girls Series (1907–08)............................	80p	£30.00
Teal Cigarettes					
		50	Cinema Stars (1930):—		
			A. Back in Blue...................................	80p	—
			B. Back in Red Brown	—	—
		30	Fish Series (1916)....................................	80p	£24.00
		50	War Incidents (1916)..................................	£1.00	£50.00
Tiger Cigarettes					
51		52	Nautch Girl Series (1911):—		
			A. Without frameline to front	£1.50	—
			B. With frameline to front		
			i) with crossed cigarettes on back	80p	£40.00
			ii) without crossed cigarettes on back	£1.00	—

E. *Printed on back No Makers Name or Brand*
(See also Imperial Tobacco Co. of Canada Ltd and United Tobacco Companies (South) Ltd)

Illus. No.	Size	Number in set		Price per card	Complete set
			Actresses "ALWICS" (1905–08):—		
		175	A. Portrait in Black..................................	£1.00	—
		50	B. Portrait in Red...................................	£3.00	—
		50	Aeroplanes (1926)....................................	60p	£30.00
45		50	Aeroplanes of Today (1936).............................	25p	£12.50
		25	Angling (1930)	60p	£15.00
		50	Arms and Armour (1910)..............................	£2.00	—
		25	Army Life	£3.00	—
		50	Art Photogravures (1913–14)............................	60p	—
		1	Australia Day (1915)..................................	—	£6.00
		22	Automobielen (1920–30)................................	£2.00	—
		75	Aviation (1910)......................................	£1.50	—
		50	Aviation Series (1911):—		
			A. With Album Clause...............................	—	—
			B. Without Album Clause.............................	80p	—
			Beauties Set I (1925):—		
	P	50	A. Black & White..................................	50p	£25.00
	MP	50	B. Coloured......................................	60p	—
	P	50	Beauties 2nd Series (1925–26):—		
			A. Black & White..................................	25p	£12.50
			B. Coloured......................................	£1.00	—
	P	50	Beauties 3rd Series (1926)	30p	£15.00
		50	Beauties Red Tinted (1905–08)	80p	—
			Beauties Tobacco Leaf Back (1905–10):—		
		52	A. With P.C. Inset.................................	80p	£40.00
		50	B. Without P.C. Inset	£2.00	£100.00
	P	50	Beauties of Great Britain (1930):—		
			A. Non Stereoscopic................................	30p	£15.00
			B. Stereoscopic...................................	80p	—
	P	50	Beautiful England (1928)...............................	20p	£10.00
	MP	60	La Belgique Monumentale et Pittoresque (1925–30)	£1.50	—
		50	Best Dogs of their Breed (1916)..........................	60p	£30.00
		50	Billiards (1929)......................................	60p	—
36		50	Birds, Beasts & Fishes (1937)..........................	16p	£8.00
	M	50	Birds, Beasts & Fishes (1929)..........................	60p	—
		24	Birds of England (1924)...............................	80p	£20.00
		50	Boy Scouts (1930) – without album clause..................	50p	£25.00
		50	Britains Defenders (1914–15):—		
			A. Blue Grey fronts.................................	70p	—
			B. Mauve fronts...................................	40p	£20.00
48		50	British Butterflies (1930)...............................	25p	£12.50
		50	British Empire Series (1913)............................	£1.00	—
		25	British Trees and Their Uses (1930)......................	70p	£17.50
		50	British Warships & Admirals (1915)	£1.25	—
		50	Butterflies & Moths (1911):—		
			A. With album clause...............................	£2.00	—
			B. Without album clause.............................	70p	—
28		50	Butterflies (Girls) (1928)	80p	£40.00
	M	50	Butterflies (Girls) (1928)	£1.00	£50.00
	M	50	Celebrities of Film & Stage (1930):—		
			A. Title on back in box..............................	40p	£20.00
			B. Title on back not in box	40p	£20.00
	LP	48	Channel Islands Past & Present (1939):—		
			A. Without "3rd Series".............................	£1.00	—
			B. With "3rd Series"..............................	13p	£5.00
25		40	Characters from the Works of Charles Dickens (1919):—		
			A. Complete Set...................................	—	£20.00
			B. 38 Different (–Nos. 33, 39)	20p	£8.00
		50	Cinema Artistes Black & White Set 1 (1928–33) (Nd 1–50)	40p	£20.00

Illus. No.	Size	Number in set		Price per card	Complete set
		50	Cinema Artistes Black & White Set 4 (1928–33) (Nd 101–150).	50p	£25.00
			Cinema Artistes Brown Set 1 (1928–33):—		
		60	A. With "Metro Golden Mayer"	40p	£24.00
		50	B. Without "Metro Golden Mayer"	60p	—
		50	Cinema Artistes Brown Set 2 (1928–33):—		
			A. Oblong Panel at Top Back	40p	£20.00
			B. Oval Panel at Top Back	60p	£30.00
	L	48	Cinema Artistes Set 3 (1928–33)	75p	
179	L	48	Cinema Celebrities (C) (1935)	25p	£12.50
	L	48	Cinema Celebrities (C) (1935)	30p	£15.00
	L	56	Cinema Celebrities (D) (1936–39)	—	£75.00
		50	Cinema Favourites (1929)	£1.50	£75.00
		50	Cinema Stars Set 2 (No. 1–50) (1928–33)	25p	£12.50
		50	Cinema Stars Set 3 (No. 51–100) (1928–33)	60p	—
		50	Cinema Stars Set 4 (No. 101–150) (1928–33)	40p	—
		100	Cinema Stars "BAMT" (Coloured) (1931)	£1.00	£100.00
	P	50	Cinema Stars Set 1 (1924–30)	40p	
	P	50	Cinema Stars Set 2 (1924–30)	30p	£15.00
	P	50	Cinema Stars Set 3 (1924–30)	50p	—
	MP	52	Cinema Stars Set 4 (1924–30)	50p	£26.00
	MP	52	Cinema Stars Set 5 (1924–30)	60p	
	MP	52	Cinema Stars Set 6 (1924–30)	£1.00	—
	LP	48	Cinema Stars Set 7 (1924–30)	—	
	P	50	Cinema Stars Set 8 (1924–30) (Nd 1–50)	50p	£25.00
	P	50	Cinema Stars Set 9 (1924–30) (Nd 51–100)	80p	£40.00
	P	50	Cinema Stars Set 10 (1924–30) (Nd 101–150)	75p	£37.50
	P	50	Cinema Stars Set 11 (1924–30) (Nd 151–200)	60p	£30.00
		25	Derby Day Series (1914)	£3.00	—
		50	Do You Know? (1923)	20p	£10.00
		50	Do You Know? 2nd Series (1931)	25p	£12.50
		25	Dracone Posthistoric (1930–40)	£4.00	—
		25	Dutch Scenes (1928)	£1.50	£37.50
35		50	Engineering Wonders (1930)	20p	£10.00
		40	English Costumes of Ten Centuries (1919)	60p	£24.00
38	P	25	English Cricketers (1926).	80p	£20.00
		26	Etchings (of Dogs) (1926)	30p	£8.00
	P	50	Famous Bridges (1935).	30p	£15.00
		50	Famous Footballers Set 1 (1923)	60p	£30.00
		50	Famous Footballers Set 2 (1924)	60p	£30.00
		50	Famous Footballers Set 3 (1925).	60p	£30.00
		25	Famous Racehorses (1926)	60p	£15.00
		25	Famous Railway Trains (1929)	80p	£20.00
		50	Favourite Flowers (1920–25)	30p	£15.00
		50	Film & Stage Favourites (1925–30)	60p	£30.00
		75	Film Favourites (1928).	50p	£37.50
		50	Flags of the Empire (1928)	40p	£20.00
174		50	Foreign Birds (1930).	20p	£10.00
		50	Game Birds & Wild Fowl (1929).	40p	£20.00
	LP	45	Grace & Beauty (Nos 1–45) (1938–39)	20p	£9.00
	LP	45	Grace & Beauty (Nos 46–90) (1938–39)	13p	£3.50
	LP	48	Guernsey, Alderney & Sark Past & Present 1st Series (1937)...	13p	£6.00
	LP	48	Guernsey, Alderney & Sark Past & Present 2nd Series (1938)..	13p	£5.00
	L	80	Guernsey Footballers Priaulx League (1938)	20p	£16.00
	P	52	Here There & Everywhere:—		
			A. Non Stereoscopic (1929)	20p	£10.00
			B. Stereoscopic (1930)	25p	£13.00
		25	Hints & Tips for Motorists (1929)	80p	£20.00
	P	50	Homeland Events (1928)	40p	£20.00
		50	Horses of Today (1906)	£2.00	—
		32	Houses of Parliament (Red Back) (1912)	60p	£19.00
		32	Houses of Parliament (Brown Backs with verse) (1912)	£4.00	—
30		50	Indian Chiefs (1930)	£1.00	£50.00
		50	Indian Regiment Series (1912)	£3.00	—
18		50	International Airliners (1937)	20p	£10.00
		25	Java Scenes (1929)	—	—
	LP	48	Jersey Then and Now 1st Series (1935)	20p	£10.00
	LP	48	Jersey Then and Now 2nd Series (1937)	13p	£5.00
		50	Jiu Jitsu (1911)	£1.00	—
202		50	Keep Fit (1939).	16p	£8.00
		50	Leaders of Men (1929)	£1.50	—
		50	Life in the Tree Tops (1931)	25p	£12.50
		50	Lighthouses (1926)	30p	£15.00
		40	London Ceremonials (1929)	50p	£20.00
	P	50	London Zoo (1927)	35p	£17.50
		50	Lucky Charms (1930)	75p	—
		25	Marvels of the Universe Series (1925–30).	80p	£20.00
206		45	Melbourne Cup Winners (1906)	£2.00	—
		50	Merchant Ships of the World (1925)	£1.50	—
		25	Merchant Ships of the World (1925)	—	—
		25	Military Portraits (1917)	£1.00	—
26		36	Modern Beauties 1st Series (1938)	14p	£5.00
200		36	Modern Beauties 2nd Series (1939)	13p	£3.00
	MP	54	Modern Beauties 1st Series (1937)	13p	£5.00
	MP	54	Modern Beauties 2nd Series (1938)	13p	£6.00
	MP	36	Modern Beauties 3rd Series (1938).	13p	£4.00
	MP	36	Modern Beauties 4th Series (1939)	13p	£3.50
	ELP	36	Modern Beauties 1st Series (1936)	50p	£18.00

Illus. No.	Size	Number in set		Price per card	Complete set
	ELP	36	Modern Beauties 2nd Series (1936)	20p	£7.50
	ELP	36	Modern Beauties 3rd Series (1937)	15p	£5.50
	ELP	36	Modern Beauties 4th Series (1937)	15p	£5.50
	ELP	36	Modern Beauties 5th Series (1938)	15p	£5.50
	ELP	36	Modern Beauties 6th Series (1938)	13p	£3.50
	ELP	36	Modern Beauties 7th Series (1938)	15p	£5.50
	LP	36	Modern Beauties 8th Series (1939)	20p	£7.50
	LP	36	Modern Beauties 9th Series (1939)	15p	£5.50
	LP	36	Modern Beauties (1939)	15p	£5.50
		50	Modern Warfare (1936)	25p	£12.50
23		25	Modes of Conveyance (1928)	60p	£15.00
		48	Motor Cars Green Back (1926)	£1.50	—
		35	Motor Cars Brown Back (1929)	—	—
		50	Motorcycles (1927)	£1.00	—
	P	50	Native Life in Many Lands (1932)	30p	£15.00
208	P	50	Natural & Man Made Wonders of the World (1937)	20p	£10.00
	P	50	Nature Studies (1928)	30p	£15.00
	P	48	Nature Studies Stereoscopic (1930)	30p	£15.00
		50	Naval Portraits (1917)	80p	—
		25	Notabilities (1917)	80p	£20.00
		25	Past & Present (1929)	60p	£15.00
197	P	48	Pictures of the East (1930):—		
			A. "A Series of 48" 17 mm long.	20p	£10.00
			B. "A Series of 48" 14 mm long.	20p	£10.00
	M	48	Picturesque China (1920–30):—		
			A. With 'P' at left of base.	50p	£25.00
			B. Without 'P' at left of base	40p	£20.00
	M	53	Playing Cards Ace of Hearts Back (1933–40)	20p	£10.00
	K	53	Playing Cards Designed Back (1933–35):—		
			A. Blue Back	50p	—
			B. Red Back.	40p	—
		36	Popular Stage, Cinema & Society Celebrities (1925–30)	£1.50	£55.00
		25	Prehistoric Animals (1931)	60p	£15.00
		50	Prominent Australian & English Cricketers (1911).	£7.50	—
		25	Puzzle Series (1916)	£1.50	£37.50
		50	Railway Working (1927)	60p	£30.00
		10	Recruiting Posters (1915)	£3.50	—
		33	Regimental Pets (1911).	£2.00	—
		50	Regimental Uniforms (1936)	50p	£25.00
32		50	Romance of the Heavens (1929)	20p	£10.00
	P	50	Round the World in Pictures Stereoscopic (1931)	30p	£15.00
		50	Royal Mail (1912)	£2.00	—
	P	50	Royal Navy (1930).	—	—
		27	Rulers of the World (1911)	—	—
		40	Safety First (1931)	30p	£12.00
29		25	Ships' Flags and Cap Badges 1st Series (1930)	60p	£15.00
		25	Ships' Flags and Cap Badges 2nd Series (1930)	60p	£15.00
	P	50	Ships and Shipping (1928).	30p	£15.00
		50	Signalling Series (1913)	£1.50	—
		100	Soldiers of the World (Tobacco Leaf Back) (1902–05)	£4.00	—
		50	Speed (1938).	30p	—
		25	Sports & Games in Many Lands (1930)	60p	£15.00
		50	Stage & Film Stars (1926)	80p	—
	M	50	Stars of Filmland (1927)	—	—
31		48	Transport Then & Now (1940)	13p	£5.00
		32	Transport of the World (1917).	—	—
24		20	Types of North American Indians (1930–40)	£2.00	—
	P	50	Types of the World (1936).	25p	£12.50
	P	270	Views of the World Stereoscopic (1908)	£1.00	—
		25	Warriors of All Nations (Gold Panel) (1937)	60p	£15.00
		50	War Incidents (Brown Back) (1915).	60p	£30.00
		50	War Incidents (Blue Back) (1916).	50p	£25.00
		50	Warships (1926)	£2.00	—
		25	Whaling (1930).	70p	£17.50
	P	50	Who's Who in Sport (1926)	50p	£25.00
		50	Wild Animals of the World (Tobacco Leaf Back) (1902–05)...	£2.00	—
		25	Wireless (1923)	80p	—
		50	Wonders of the Past (1930)	40p	£20.00
19		50	Wonders of the Sea (1929).	30p	£15.00
203		25	Wonders of the World (1925–30)	20p	£5.00
14		40	World Famous Cinema Artistes (1933)	40p	£16.00
	M	40	World Famous Cinema Artistes (1933).	40p	£16.00
		50	World's Products	20p	£10.00
	P	50	The World of Sport (1927)	50p	£25.00
	P	50	Zoo (1935)	30p	£15.00
		50	Zoological Studies (1928):—		
			A. Brown Back	30p	£15.00
			B. Black Back	—	—

F. Plain Backs

		50	Actors & Actresses "WALP" (1905–08):—		
			A. Portraits in Black & White, Glossy.	80p	£40.00
			B. Portraits Flesh Tinted, Matt.	80p	£40.00
		50	Actresses "ALWICS" (1905–08).	£1.50	—
		50	Actresses, Four Colours Surround (1903–08).	60p	£30.00
		30	Actresses Unicoloured (1908–13):—		
			A. Fronts in Purple Brown	40p	£12.00
			B. Fronts in Light Brown	40p	£12.00
		50	Animals & Birds (1912)	80p	£40.00

Illus. No.	Size	Number in set		Price per card	Complete set
		60	Animals – Cut Outs (1912)	50p	—
		50	Art Photogravures (1912)	£1.00	—
		50	Aviation Series (1911)...............................	£1.50	—
		40	Beauties Brown Tinted (1913)	60p	—
		50	Beauties with Backgrounds (1911)	80p	—
		32	Beauties Picture Hats I with borders (1914)	60p	£19.00
		45	Beauties Picture Hats II without borders (1914)	60p	—
		30	Beauties & Children (1910–15)	£3.00	—
		30	Beauties "Celebrated Actresses" (1910–15)...........	£1.00	—
		52	Birds of Brilliant Plumage P.C. Inset (1914)	80p	—
		25	Bonzo Series (1923):—		
			A. With Series Title	70p	£17.50
			B. Without Series Title	80p	—
		30	Boy Scouts Signalling (1920–25):—		
			A. Captions in English	80p	£24.00
			B. Captions in Siamese...........................	80p	£24.00
		50	British Man of War Series (1910)	£3.00	—
		50	Butterflies & Moths (1910)	60p	—
		50	Cinema Artistes (1928–33)	—	—
		50	Cinema Stars (1925–35) RB21/259:—		
			A. Front Matt	40p	£20.00
			B. Front Glossy	60p	—
		50	Cinema Stars (1925–35) RB21/260 (Nd. 1–50).........	40p	—
		50	Cinema Stars (1925–35) RB21/260 (Nd. 51–100).......	60p	—
		50	Cinema Stars (1925–35) RB21/260 (Nd. 101–150)	60p	—
		100	Cinema Stars (1925–35) RB21/260 (Nd. 201–300)	30p	£30.00
		50	Cinema Stars "FLAG" (1925–35)	50p	—
		27	Dancing Girls (1913)..............................	£1.00	—
		32	Drum Horses (1910)	£1.50	—
		50	English Period Costumes............................	50p	£25.00
		50	Flag Girls of All Nations (1911)	80p	—
			Flags Pennons & Signals (1905–10):—		
		70	A. Numbered 1–70...............................	50p	—
		70	B. Unnumbered	30p	—
		50	C. Numbered 71–120	40p	—
		45	D. Numbered 121–165	60p	—
		20	Flowers (1915).....................................	50p	£10.00
		50	Girls of All Nations (1908)	75p	—
		30	Heroic Deeds (1913)	75p	£22.50
		25	Hindou Gods (1909)................................	£2.00	—
		32	Houses of Parliament (1914)	£1.25	—
		25	Indian Mogul Paintings (1909)	—	—
168		53	Jockeys & Owners Colours P.C. Inset.................	75p	—
		30	Merrie England Female Studies (1922)................	£3.00	—
	K	36	Modern Beauties 1st Series (1938)	—	—
		36	Modern Beauties 2nd Series (1939)	—	—
	P	48	Movie Stars (1925–30)	50p	—
		50	Music Hall Celebrities (1911):—		
			A. Blue Border	£1.50	—
			B. Gilt Border	£1.00	—
			C. Red Border	£1.50	—
			D. Yellow Border	£3.00	—
	P	50	New Zealand, Early Scenes & Maori Life (1925–30)	—	—
		50	Poultry & Pidgeons (1925–30)	—	—
		25	Products of the World (1914)........................	50p	£12.50
		50	Royal Mail (1912)	—	—
22		36	Ships & Their Pennants (1913).......................	75p	—
		75	Soldiers of the World (1900–05)	£2.00	—
		30	Sporting Girls (1913)	£1.00	—
		50	Sports of the World (1917):—		
			A. Brown Front	—	—
			B. Coloured Front................................	60p	—
	M	50	Stars of Filmland (1927)	—	—
		32	Transport of the World (1917).......................	50p	£16.00
		50	Types of the British Army (1908):—		
			A. Numbered....................................	£1.00	—
			B. Unnumbered	80p	—
	P	50	Types of the World (1936)...........................	—	—
	P	50	Units of the British Army & RAF (1925–30)	—	—
	M	50	Women of Nations (Flag Girls) (1922)	80p	—

G. Paper Backed Silks issued 1910–1917

	Size	Number in set		Price per card	Complete set
	M	25	Arabic Proverbs	£6.00	—
	M	50	Arms of the British Empire:—		
			A. Back in Blue...................................	£1.00	—
			B. Back in Brown.................................	£2.00	—
	M	50	Australian Wild Flowers	£1.00	—
	M	50	Best Dogs of their Breed	£1.00	—
		110	Crests & Badges of the British Army.................	£2.00	—
	M	108	Crests & Badges of the British Army.................	£1.00	—
	M	50	Crests & Colours of Australian Universities, Colleges & Schools	£1.00	—

BRITISH AMERICAN TOBACCO COMPANY (CHINA) LTD. ___

		Number in set		Price per card	Complete set
		32	Sectional Picture – "Beauties of Old China" (1934)	£2.00	—

BRITISH AMERICAN TOBACCO CO. LTD., Switzerland

Illus. No.	Size	Number in set		Price per card	Complete set
		30	Series Actrices (1921)	£3.00	—

BROWN & WILLIAMSON TOBACCO CORP., U.S.A. (WINGS CIGARETTES)

21	M	50	Modern American Airplanes (1930's):—		
			A. Inscribed "Series A"	80p	—
			B. Without "Series A"	60p	£30.00
	M	50	Modern American Airplanes "Series B" (1930's)	60p	£30.00
	M	50	Modern American Airplanes "Series C" (1930's)	60p	£30.00

D. BUCHNER & CO. U.S.A.

		48	Actors (1885–92)	£6.00	—
	L	50	Actresses (1885–92)	£7.50	—
		144	Baseball Players (1885–92)	£15.00	—
	L	28	Butterflies & Bugs (1885–92)	£10.00	—
183	L	52	Morning Glory Maidens (1885–92)	£12.50	—
	L	23	Musical Instruments (1885–92)	£15.00	—
	L	21	Yacht Club Colours (1885–92)	£15.00	—

BUCKTROUT & CO. LTD., Guernsey. Chanel Islands

	M	416	Around the World (1926–27):—		
			A. Inscribed "Places of Interest" Nd. 1–104	25p	£26.00
			B. Inscribed "Around the World" Nd. 105–208	25p	£26.00
			C. Inscribed "Around the World" Nd. 209–312	25p	£26.00
			D. Inscribed "Around the World" Nd. 313–416	25p	£26.00
		24	Birds of England (1923)	80p	£20.00
		50	Cinema Stars 1st Series (1921)	40p	£20.00
		50	Cinema Stars 2nd Series (1922)	60p	£30.00
	M	50	Football Teams (1924)	50p	£25.00
13	M	22	Football Teams of the Bailiwick (1924)	24p	£5.00
		123	Guernsey Footballers (1910–15)	75p	—
16		20	Inventors Series (1924)	14p	£2.75
		25	Marvels of the Universe Series (1923)	60p	£15.00
	M	53	Playing Cards (1928–29)	30p	£15.00
		25	Sports & Pastimes (1925)	80p	—

CALCUTTA CIGARETTE CO. India

		25	Actresses "ALWICS" (1905–08):—		
			A. Fronts in Blue	£5.00	—
			B. Fronts in chocolate	£7.00	£175.00

A. G. CAMERON & SIZER, U.S.A. (including Cameron & Cameron)

		25	The New Discovery:—		
			A. Without Overprint.................................	£7.50	—
			B. With Overprint	£7.50	—
178		24	Occupations, For Women..............................	£15.00	—
			Photographic Cards		
		?1	Actresses...	£5.00	—
	L	?2	Actresses...	—	—
		343	Framed Paintings	£2.00	—

V. CAMILLERI, Malta

	MP	104	Popes of Rome (1922):—		
			A. Nd. 1–52	60p	£30.00
			B. Nd. 53–104	60p	£30.00

CAMLER TOBACCO COY Malta

	P	?239	Footballers (1920–30)...................................	—	—
	M	96	Maltese Families Coats of Arms:—		
			A. Thick Board (1920–30)............................	40p	—
			B. Thin Board (1958–59).............................	75p	—

CARRERAS LTD., Australia

		72	Film Star Series (1933)	60p	—
		72	Football Series (1933)....................................	60p	—
		24	Personality Series (1933)	75p	—
		72	Personality Series Film Stars (1933)......................	50p	—
15		72	Personality Series Footballers (1933)	75p	—

CHING & CO. Jersey, Channel Islands

Illus. No.	Size	Number in set		Price per card	Complete set
	L	24	Around & About in Jersey, 1st Series (1964).................	8p	£2.00
	L	24	Around & About in Jersey, 2nd Series (1964).................	80p	—
159		25	Do You Know (1962)...............................	7p	50p
			Album.....................................•......	—	60p
		48	Flowers (1962)...................................	60p	£30.00
184	L	24	Jersey Past & Present 1st Series (1960)	7p	70p
	L	24	Jersey Past & Present 2nd Series (1962)...............	8p	£2.00
			Album for 1st & 2nd series Combined................	—	80p
180	L	24	Jersey Past & Present 3rd Series (1963)	7p	70p
			Album..	—	75p
161		25	Ships & Their Workings (1961).....................	7p	50
		50	Veteran & Vintage Cars (1960)	10p	£5.00
			Album..	—	£1.25

W. A. & A. C. CHURCHMAN, Channel Islands

(All cards without ITC clause)

	Size	Number in set			Complete set
	M	48	Air Raid Precautions (1938).......................	—	£20.00
	M	48	Holidays in Britain (Sepia) (1937)...................	—	£20.00
	M	48	Holidays in Britain (Coloured) (1938)................	—	£20.00
	M	48	Modern Wonders (1938):—		
			A. ITC Clause blocked out in Silver....................	—	—
			B. Reprinted without ITC Clause..................	—	—
	M	48	The Navy at Work (1937).........................	—	£20.00
	M	48	The RAF at Work (1939)	—	£20.00
	M	48	Wings Over the Empire (1939).....................	—	£20.00

THE CIGARETTE COMPANY, Jersey, Channel Islands

		72	Jersey Footballers (1908–14)	£1.50	—

C. COLOMBOS, Malta

Illus. No.	Size	Number in set		Price per card	Complete set
	MP	200	Actresses (Pre 1918)	—	—
	MP	44	Actresses (Pre 1918)	—	—
		50	Actresses Coloured (Pre 1918)	—	—
	MP	55	Celebrities (Pre 1918)	—	—
	P	136	Dante's Devine Comedy (Pre 1918)	—	—
			Famous Oil Paintings (Pre 1918):—		
	MP	72	1) Series A................................	50p	—
	MP	108	2) Series B................................	50p	—
	MP	240	3) Series C................................	50p	—
	MP	100	4) Series D................................	50p	—
	LP	91	5) Large size..............................	£2.00	—
	MP	100	Life of Napoleon Bonaparte (Pre 1918)	75p	—
10	MP	70	Life of Nelson (Pre 1918)..........................	75p	—
	MP	70	Life of Wellington (Pre 1918).......................	75p	—
	MP	100	National Types and Costumes (Pre 1918)	75p	—
	MP	20	Opera Singers (Pre 1918)	—	—
		120	Paintings and Statues (Pre 1918)....................	25p	£30.00
	M	112	Royalty & Celebrities (Pre 1918)....................	75p	—

D. CONDACHI & SON, Malta

11		?25	Beauties (1900–1910)	£5.00	—

CONSOLIDATED CIGARETTE CO., U.S.A.

		25	Ladies of the White House:—		
			A. Size 73 × 43 mm White borders	£12.50	—
			B. Size 70 × 38 mm No borders	£10.00	—

COPE BROS. & CO., LTD.

A. Indian Issue

		30	Flags of Nations (1896–1905)	£8.00	—

B. Danish Issues

		50	Jordklodens Hunde (1905–13)............................	—	—
		30	Scandinavian Actors & Actresses (1905–13).................	£6.00	—
		35	Speider Billeder I Hver Pakke (1905–13)...................	—	—
		25	Uniformer A F Fremgrende Britiske Regimenter (1905–13)..	—	—
		25	Vilde Dyr Og Fugle (1905–13)	—	—

A. G. COUSIS & CO. Malta

Illus. No.	Size	Number in set		Price per card	Complete set
			Actors & Actresses (Pre 1918):—		
	P	100	A. Back with Framework	—	—
	KP	100	B. Back without Framework	—	—
207	K	254	Actors & Actresses (1920–30)......................	25p	—
	KP	100	Actresses Series I (Pre 1918)	—	—

Illus. No.	Size	Number in set		Price per card	Complete set
	KP	80	Actresses Series II (Pre 1918)	—	—
	P	100	Actresses (Pre 1918):—		
			A. Series I.	50p	—
			B. Series II.	60p	—
			C. Series III.	60p	—
			D. Series IV.	50p	—
			E. Series V.	70p	—
			F. Series VI.	70p	—
			G. Series VII.	70p	—
			H. Series VIII	—	—
			I. Series IX.	70p	—
			J. Series X.	70p	—
			K. Series XI.	70p	—
			L. Series XII.	70p	—
			M. Series XIII	70p	—
			N. Series XIV	50p	—
			O. Series XV	60p	—
			P. Series XVI	70p	—
			Q. Series XVII	60p	—
			R. Series XVIII	70p	—
			S. Series XIX	—	—
			Actresses (Pre 1918):—		
	KP	1895	A. Miniature Size 50 × 30 mm	25p	—
	P	1160	B. Small Size 58 × 39 mm.	30p	—
	MP	248	Actresses, Celebrities & Warships (Pre 1918)	—	—
			Actresses, Partners & National Costumes (Pre 1918):—		
	KP	200	A. Miniature size 50 × 30 mm.	75p	—
	P	100	B. Small Size 60 × 39 mm.	75p	—
	MP	50	Beauties, Couples & Children (Pre 1918):—		
			A. Back inscribed "Collection No. 1"	75p	—
			B. Back inscribed "Collection No. 2"	75p	—
			C. Back inscribed "Collection No. 3"	75p	—
	K	50	Beauties, Couples & Children (Red Back) (1920–30)	75p	—
	P	402	Celebrities Numbered Matt (Pre 1918):—		
			A. Front inscribed "Cousis's Dubec Cigarettes" Nd. 1–300	30p	—
			B. Front inscribed "Cousis's Cigarettes" Nd. 301–402	—	—
	P	2161	Celebrities Unnumbered (Pre 1918):—		
			A. Miniature size 50 × 30 mm.	25p	—
			B. Small size 59 × 39 mm	25p	—
	MP	72	Grand Masters of the Order of Jerusalem (Pre 1918)	—	—
	P	100	National Costumes (Pre 1918)	75p	—
	MP	?57	Paris Exhibition 1900 (Pre 1918)	—	—
	MP	102	Paris Series (Pre 1918).	—	—
			Popes of Rome (Pre 1918):—		
	MP	182	A. Back inscribed "A.G. Cousis' Dubec Cigarettes"	40p	—
	MP	81	B. Back inscribed "Cousis' Dubec Cigarettes".	80p	—
	P	100	Statues & Monuments (Pre 1918):—		
			A. Numbered.	75p	—
			B. Unnumbered	75p	—
	KP	127	Views of Malta (Pre 1918).	50p	—
	P	115	Views of Malta Numbered (Pre 1918).	50p	—
	MP	127	Views of Malta Numbered (Pre 1918).	40p	—
	MP	?65	Views of Malta Unnumbered (Pre 1918)	50p	—
	P	555	Views of the World (Pre 1918):—		
			A. Small size 59 × 39 mm	30p	—
			B. Medium size 65 × 45 mm	60p	—
	P	99	Warships White border (Pre 1918).	£1.00	—
			Warships, Liners & Other Vessels (Pre 1918):—		
	MP	64	A. "Cousis' Dubec Cigarettes"	80p	—
	MP	22	B. "Cousis' Excelsior Cigarettes".	£1.00	—
	MP	37	C. "Cousis' Superior Cigarettes"	£2.00	—
20	MP	850	D. "Cousis' Cigarettes"	40p	—
	KP	850	E. "Cousis' Cigarettes"	30p	—

CROWN TOBACCO CO. India

12		?15	National Types, Costumes & Flags (1895–1905)	£15.00	—

DIXSON, Australia

		50	Australian MP's and Celebrities (1900–1902).	£4.00	—

DOMINION TOBACCO CO., Canada

		50	The Smokers of the World (1900–05)	£6.00	—

DOMINION TOBACCO CO. LTD., New Zealand

		50	Coaches & Coaching Days (1925–30)	70p	—
		50	People and Places Famous in New Zealand History (1925–30)	80p	—
		50	Products of the World (1925–30)	40p	£20.00
3		50	U.S.S. Co.'s Steamers (1925–30).	90p	—

DUDGEON & ARNELL, Australia

Illus. No.	Size	Number in set		Price per card	Complete set
	K	16	1934 Australian Test Team (1934)	£1.25	£20.00
	K	55	Famous Ships (1933).................................	£1.00	—

W. DUKE SONS & CO., U.S.A.

Illus. No.	Size	Number in set		Price per card	Complete set
	EL	?	Actors & Actresses (Photographic) RB23/–D76–81...........	75p	—
		50	Actors & Actresses Series No. 1............................	£4.00	—
		50	Actors & Actresses Series No. 2............................	£4.00	—
		25	Actresses RB18/27......................................	£5.00	—
	EL	?	Actresses, Celebrities & Children (Photographic).............	£1.00	—
	EL	25	Albums of America Stars.................................	£10.00	—
	EL	25	Battle Scenes...	£6.00	—
	EL	25	Breeds of Horses.......................................	£6.00	—
	EL	25	Bridges..	£6.00	—
2	EL	25	Comic Characters	£5.00	—
		50	Coins of All Nations....................................	£4.00	—
	EL	25	Cowboy Scenes...	£7.50	—
	EL	50	Fairest Flowers in the World	£6.00	—
		50	Fancy Dress Ball Costumes	£3.00	£150.00
	EL	50	Fancy Dress Ball Costumes	£7.50	—
		50	Fishers and Fish	£4.00	£200.00
	EL	25	Flags & Costumes	£7.50	—
		50	Floral Beauties & Language of Flowers	£5.00	—
172	EL	25	French Novelties	£6.00	—
	EL	25	Gems of Beauty	£6.00	—
		50	Great Americans	£5.00	—
		25	Gymnastic Exercises....................................	—	—
	EL	25	Habitations of Man.....................................	£5.00	—
		50	Histories of Generals (Booklets).........................	£6.00	—
		50	Histories of Poor Boys who have become rich & other famous people	£7.00	—
		50	Holidays	£4.00	£200.00
173	EL	25	Illustrated Songs.......................................	£6.00	—
	EL	25	Industries of the States.................................	—	—
		50	Jokes..	£5.00	—
	EL	25	Lighthouses (Die Cut)	£6.00	—
	EL	25	Miniature Novelties	£6.00	—
8		50	Musical Instruments....................................	£5.00	—
		36	Ocean & River Steamers	£6.00	—
	M	240	Photographs from Life RB23/76–84.......................	£2.00	—
		53	Playing Cards	£5.00	—
		50	Popular Songs & Dancers	£6.00	—
		50	Postage Stamps..	£6.00	—
			Rulers Flags & Coats of Arms (1888):—		
	EL	50	A. Thick Card Type..............................	£6.00	—
	EL	50	B. Thin Folders	£4.00	—
		50	Scenes of Perilous Occupations...........................	£5.00	—
	EL	25	Sea Captains	£8.00	—
		50	Shadows	£4.00	£200.00
	EL	25	Snap Shots from Puck	£5.00	—
	EL	25	Stars of the Stage 1st Series:—		
			A. With Duke...................................	£5.00	£125.00
			B. Inscribed "3rd Series"........................	£6.00	—
139	EL	25	Stars of the Stage 2nd Series	£6.00	—
	EL	25	Stars of the Stage 3rd Series	£5.00	£125.00
	EL	25	Stars of the Stage 4th Series (Die Cut)....................	£6.00	—
	EL	48	State Governors, Coats of Arms..........................	£7.50	—
	EL	48	State Governors, Coats of Arms (Folders)	£4.00	—
		50	The Terrors of America & Their Doings	£5.00	—
	EL	50	The Terrors of America & Their Doings	£7.50	—
		50	Tinted Photos:—		
			A. Standard size	£7.50	—
			B. Die Cut to Shape	£8.00	—
	EL	25	Types of Vessels (Die Cut)	£6.00	—
		50	Vehicles of the World...................................	£6.00	£300.00
		50	Yacht Colours of the World..............................	£4.00	—

Photographic Cards

Illus. No.	Size	Number in set		Price per card	Complete set
		340	Actors & Actresses "Cross-Cut Cigarettes" with number and caption in design Group 1..............................	£1.00	—
		260	Actors & Actresses "Cross-Cut Cigarettes" in design, number and caption at base Group 2................................	£1.00	—
		?	Actors & Actresses "Cross-Cut Cigarettes" and all wording at base Group 3...	£1.00	—
		148	Actors & Actresses "Dukes Cameo Cigarettes" in design, number and caption at base Group 4	£1.00	—
		?	Actors & Actresses "Dukes Cameo Cigarettes" number and caption at base Group 5................................	£1.00	—
		?	Actors & Actresses "Dukes Cigarettes" in design, number and caption at base Group 6................................	£1.00	—
		?	Actors & Actresses "Dukes Cigarettes" and all wording at base Group 7...	£1.00	—
		?	Actors, Actresses & Celebrities. Printed Back:—		
			1. Horizontal "Dukes Cameo Cigarettes" back...........	£1.00	—
			2. Vertical "Sales 1888" back	—	—
			3. Horizontal "Dukes Cigarettes" back	75p	—

H. ELLIS & CO., U.S.A.

Illus. No.	Size	Number in set		Price per card	Complete set
		25	Breeds of Dogs	£8.00	—
		25	Costumes of Women..	—	—
		25	Generals of the Late Civil War	—	—
		25	Photographic Cards – Actresses	—	—

G. W. GAIL & AX., U.S.A.

Illus. No.	Size	Number in set		Price per card	Complete set
	EL	25	Battle Scenes	£8.00	—
	EL	25	Bicycle & Trick Riders	—	—
	EL	25	French Novelties	£8.00	—
	EL	25	Industries of States	£8.00	—
	EL	25	Lighthouses (Die Cut)	—	—
138	EL	25	Novelties (Die Cut)	£10.00	—
	EL	?	Photographic Cards	£1.50	—
	EL	25	Stars of the Stage	£7.50	—

GENERAL CIGAR COMPANY, Montreal, Canada

Illus. No.	Size	Number in set		Price per card	Complete set
6	EL	36	Northern Birds (1968)	50p	—

GOODWIN & CO., U.S.A.

Illus. No.	Size	Number in set		Price per card	Complete set
		15	Beauties "PAC"	—	—
		50	Champions..	£6.00	—
		50	Dogs of the World	£3.00	—
		50	Flowers	£5.00	—
7		50	Games & Sports Series	£6.00	—
		50	Holidays	—	—
		50	Occupations for Women	£20.00	—
			Photographic Cards		
		?	Actors & Actresses	£1.00	—
		?	Baseball Players	£15.00	—
		?	Celebrities & Prizefighters.........................	£3.00	—
		50	Vehicles of the World	£8.00	—

GUERNSEY TOBACCO CO., Channel Islands

Illus. No.	Size	Number in set		Price per card	Complete set
			A Famous Picture:—		
		49	A. And When Did You Last See Your Father? (1934)......	50p	£25.00
		48	B. The Laughing Cavalier (1935)	50p	£24.00
		48	C. The Toast (1936)...................................	50p	£24.00
	K	52	Miniature Playing Cards (1933–36).........................	40p	—

THOS. H. HALL, U.S.A.

Illus. No.	Size	Number in set		Price per card	Complete set
		4	Actresses RB23/–H6–1.....................................	£40.00	—
		14	Actresses RB23/–H6–2.....................................	£10.00	—
		140	Actors & Actresses RB23/–H6–3	£10.00	—
		112	Actresses & Actors RB23/–H6–4	£10.00	—
		?	Actresses & Actors RB23/–H6–5	£10.00	—
		?	Actresses & Actors RB23/–H6–6	£10.00	—
		49	Actresses RB23/–H6–7....................................	—	—
		11	Actresses RB23/–H6–8....................................	—	—
		25	Actresses RB23/–H6–9....................................	£12.50	—
		11	Actresses RB23/–H6–10	—	—
		12	Athletes RB23/H6–3.....................................	—	—
		4	Presidental Candidates RB23/H6–1	—	—
94		22	Presidents of the United States RB23/H6–11	£10.00	—
		25	Theatrical Types RB23/H6–12	£15.00	—

HIGNETT BROS. & CO., New Zealand

Illus. No.	Size	Number in set		Price per card	Complete set
	MP	50	Beauties Set 1 (1926):—		
			A. Back without Framelines no brand mentioned..........	£1.00	—
			B. Back with Framelines "Chess Cigarettes"	50p	£25.00
	MP	50	Beauties Set 2 (1927).................................	75p	—

R. & J. HILL LTD.

Illus. No.	Size	Number in set		Price per card	Complete set
		10	Chinese Series (1911–17)	£6.00	—

Illus. No.	Size	Number in set		Price per card	Complete set
	EL	25	National Types (1898–1901).............................	£5.00	—

IMPERIAL TOBACCO COMPANY OF CANADA LTD., Canada —

A. With Firms Name

		25	Beauties – Girls in Costume (1903–05)......................	—	—
		24	Beauties – Smoke Girls (1903–05).........................	—	—
	M	50	Birds, Beasts & Fishes (1923–24).........................	80p	£40.00
	L	100	Birds of Canada (1924).................................	£1.25	—
	L	100	Birds of Canada (Western Canada)........................	—	—
		50	British Birds (1923)...................................	35p	£17.50
4		48	Canadian History Series (1926)..........................	50p	—
		50	Children of All Nations (1924)...........................	35p	£17.50
		23	Dogs Series (1924)...................................	50p	£12.00
		50	Dogs 2nd Series (1925)................................	50p	—
		50	Famous English Actresses (1924).........................	50p	£25.00
		50	Film Favourites (1925–6):—		
			A. English Issue:—		
			i) Numbered...........................	£1.00	—
			ii) Unnumbered.........................	£1.50	—
			B. French Issue:—		
			i) Numbered...........................	£3.00	—
			ii) Unnumbered.........................	—	—
		50	Fish & Bait (1924)....................................	50p	£25.00
1		50	Fishes of the World (1924)..............................	60p	£30.00
		50	Flower Culture in Pots (1925)...........................	40p	£20.00
		30	Game Bird Series (1925)...............................	50p	£15.00
		50	Gardening Hints (1923)................................	35p	£17.50
	M	25	Heraldic Signs & Their Origins (1925).....................	60p	£15.00
9		50	How to Play Golf (1925)...............................	£1.25	—
		50	Infantry Training (1915):—		
			A. Glossy Card......................	80p	—
			B. Matt Card.......................	80p	—
	L	48	Mail Carriers and Stamps (1903–5).......................	—	—
5		50	Merchant Ships of the World (1924).......................	40p	£20.00
		25	Military Portraits (1914–15).............................	£1.00	—
		50	Modern War Weapons 'Sweet Caporal" issue (1914–15)......	£1.00	—
101		56	Motor Cars (1924)....................................	80p	£45.00
		50	Naval Portraits (1914–15)..............................	£1.00	—
		25	Notabilities (1914–15).................................	£1.00	—
		53	Poker Hands (1924)...................................	60p	—
		53	Poker Hands New Series (1925)..........................	60p	—
		25	Poultry Alphabet (1924)................................	60p	—
		50	Railway Engines (1924):—		
			A. With Wills Blanked Out................	80p	—
			B. Without Wills......................	50p	£25.00
		50	The Reason Why......................................	50p	£25.00
		127	Smokers Golf Cards (1925–26)..........................	£1.25	—

B. Without Firms Name

		50	Arms of the British Empire (1911)........................	£1.00	—
		50	Around the World (1910–15).............................	£2.00	—
		100	Baseball Series (1912).................................	—	—
		30	Bird Series (1910–15)..................................	—	—
		50	Boy Scouts (1911) – with album clause....................	£1.25	—
		50	Canadian Historical Portraits (1913–15)...................	£2.50	—
		50	Canadian History Series (1914)..........................	60p	—
		50	Fish Series (1910–15)..................................	—	—
		50	Fowls, Pigeons and Dogs (1911).........................	£1.00	—
		45	Hockey Players (1912).................................	£1.50	—
		36	Hockey Series Coloured (1911)..........................	£3.00	—
		50	How to do it (1910–15).................................	£2.00	—
171		100	Lacrosse Series Leading Players (1910–15).................	£1.00	—
		100	Lacrosse Series Coloured (1910–15).......................	£1.25	—
		50	Lacrosse Series Black & White (1910–15)...................	£1.25	—
		50	L'Historie Du Canada (1926)............................	80p	—
		50	Movie Stars..	60p	—
	L	50	Pictures of Canadian Life (1910–15):—		
			A. Brown Front......................	—	—
			B. Green Front......................	£3.00	—
		50	Prominent Men of Canada (1910–15)......................	£1.50	—
		50	Tricks & Puzzles (1910–15).............................	£5.00	—
		50	Types of Nations....................................	—	—
103		25	V.C. Heroes (Blue Back) (1915)..........................	80p	£20.00
	L	45	Views of the World (1910–15)...........................	—	—
		25	The Worlds Dreadnoughts (1910).........................	£1.00	—

C. Silks Issued 1910–25

	M	55	Animals with Flags...................................	£1.50	—
	EL	50	Canadian History Series...............................	£4.00	—
	M	121	Canadian Miscellany..................................	£1.50	—
	M	55	Garden Flowers of the World............................	£1.00	£55.00
	M	55	Orders & Military Medals...............................	£1.50	—
	M	55	Regimental Uniforms of Canada..........................	£1.50	—
	M	50	Yachts Pennants & Views...............................	£1.50	—

THE IMPERIAL TOBACCO CO. OF INDIA LTD., India

Illus. No.	Size	Number in set		Price per card	Complete set
102		25	Indian Historical Views (1915):—		
			A. Set 1 First Arrangement...............................	80p	£20.00
			B. Set 2 Second Arrangement	80p	£20.00
		40	Nautch Girl Series:—		
			A. "Pedro Cigarettes" (1905–09)	£1.00	—
			B. "Railway Cigarettes" (1907–08)	£1.00	—
		52	Nautch Girl Series, P.C. Inset:—		
			A. "Pedro Cigarettes" (1905–09)	£1.00	£52.00
			B. "Railway Cigarettes" (1907–08)	£1.00	—
	K	53	Playing Cards Red Back (1919–20)	50p	—
	K	52	Playing Cards Blue Back (1933)	—	—

THE JERSEY TOBACCO CO. LTD., Channel Islands

	Size	Number		Price	Complete
	K	53	Miniature Playing Cards (1933)	40p	£20.00

JUST SO, U.S.A.

	Size	Number		Price	Complete
	EL	?	Actresses (1885–95).......................................	£3.00	—

KENTUCKY TOBACCO PTY. LTD., South Africa

	Size	Number		Price	Complete
	L	120	The March of Mankind (1940)	75p	—

WM. S. KIMBALL & CO., U.S.A.

Illus. No.	Size	Number		Price	Complete
		?25	Actresses	—	—
		72	Ancient Coins	£8.00	—
95		48	Arms of Dominions..	£6.00	—
		50	Ballet Queens..	£5.00	—
		52	Beauties with Playing Card Insets.........................	£6.00	—
	EL	20	Beautiful Bathers..	£8.00	—
97		50	Butterflies	£5.00	—
		50	Champions of Games & Sports	£7.50	—
		50	Dancing Girls of the World	£5.00	—
		50	Dancing Women	£4.00	—
		50	Fancy Bathers...	£4.00	—
		50	Goddesses of the Greeks & Romans	—	—
	EL	25	Household Pets..	£7.00	—
		?	Photographic Actresses RB23/K26–15–2	£2.00	—
	EL	20	Pretty Athletes	£8.00	—
		50	Savage & Semi Barbarous Chiefs and Rulers	£7.50	—

KINNEY BROS., U.S.A.

Illus. No.	Size	Number		Price	Complete
		25	Actresses Group 1 Set 1 RB18/1	£3.00	£75.00
		25	Actresses Group 1 Set 2 RB18/2	£5.00	—
		25	Actresses Group 1 Set 3 RB18/3	£7.50	—
		25	Actresses Group 1 Set 4	—	—
		25	Actresses Group 1 Set 5	—	—
		25	Actresses Group 2 RB18/15	£4.00	—
		25	Actresses Group 2 RB18/16:—		
			A. Subjects named	£3.00	—
			B. Subjects unnamed	£2.00	—
		25	Actresses Group 3 RB18/26	£2.00	—
		25	Actresses Group 3 RB18/29	£2.00	—
		50	Actresses Group 4 RB18/36	£2.00	—
		150	Actresses Group 4	—	—
		25	Animals..	£4.00	—
		10	Butterflies of the World Light background	£5.00	—
96		50	Butterflies of the World Gold background	£3.50	—
		25	Famous Gems of the World	£4.00	£100.00
		52	Harlequin Cards 1st Series	£6.00	—
		53	Harlequin Cards 2nd Series	£6.00	—
	L	50	International Cards..	£10.00	—
	K	24	Jocular Oculars...	—	—
		25	Leaders:—		
			A. Standard size	£4.00	£100.00
			B. Narrow card – officially cut	£4.00	£100.00
		50	Magic Changing Cards	£6.00	—
		622	Military Series...	£1.50	—
		50	National Dances:—		
			A. Front with white border............................	£4.00	£200.00
			B. Front without border	£5.00	—
		25	Naval Vessels of the World................................	£6.00	—
		25	Novelties Type 1 Thick Circular No border	£10.00	—
		50	Novelties Type 2 Thin Circular with border	£4.00	—
			Novelties Type 3 Die Cut		
		25	A. Inscribed "25 Styles"...............................	£3.00	—
106		50	B. Inscribed "50 Styles"...............................	£3.00	—
		75	C. Inscribed "75 Styles"..............................	£3.00	—
		50	Novelties Type 5 Standard Size Cases Die Cut..............	£5.00	—

KINNEY BROS., U.S.A. (continued)

Illus. No.	Size	Number in set		Price per card	Complete set
		?11	Novelties Type 6 Oval..	£12.50	—
			Photographic Cards		
		?	A. Actors & Actresses Horizontal Back with Kinneys Name	75p	
		?	B. Actors & Actresses Vertical Sweet Caporal Backs.......	50p	
		45	C. Famous Ships	£4.00	
			Racehorses:—		
		25	1. American Horses:—		
			A. Back with series title "Famous Running Horses"	£4.00	
			B. Back "Return 25 of these small cards" 11 lines of text	£4.00	
		25	2. English Horses "Return 25 of these cards" with 6 lines of text	£3.00	£75.00
		25	3. Great American Trotters.............................	£6.00	—
107		50	Surf Beauties	£5.00	£250.00
		52	Transparent Playing Cards.................................	£7.50	—
		25	Types of Nationalities (Folders)	£8.00	—

KRAMERS TOBACCO CO. (PTY.) LTD., South Africa

		50	Badges of South African Rugby Football Clubs (1933)	£1.25	—

LAMBERT & BUTLER

Illus. No.	Size	Number in set		Price per card	Complete set
		50	Actors & Actresses "WALPS" (1905)......................	£1.00	—
		250	Actresses "ALWICS" (1905–6):—		
			A. Portraits in Black, Border in Red	£1.00	
			B. Portraits and Border in Black......................	£2.00	
		50	Beauties Red Tinted (1906–10)	£1.50	
		83	Danske Byvaabner (1910–15)	£5.00	
	M	26	Etchings of Dogs (1926)..................................	—	—
		25	Flag Girls of All Nations (1908)	£3.00	
	P	50	Homeland Events (1928).................................	60p	£30.00
	P	50	London Zoo (1927)......................................	£1.00	—
		50	Merchant Ships of the World (1924)	80p	
		30	Music Hall Celebrities (1916).............................	£1.50	
100	P	50	Popular Film Stars (1926):—		
			A. Series title in one line, no brand quoted................	50p	£25.00
			B. Series title in two lines inscribed "Varsity Cigarettes" ...	£1.00	—
			C. Series title in two lines no brand quoted	50p	£25.00
	P	50	The Royal Family at Home & Abroad (1927)	40p	£20.00
		100	Royalty, Notabilities and Events in Russia, China, Japan and South Africa (1900–02)	£3.50	—
		100	Russo Japanese Series (1905).............................	£2.00	—
	P	50	Types of Modern Beauty (1927)	60p	—
108	P	50	Who's Who in Sport (1926)	60p	£30.00
	P	50	The World of Sport (1927)	40p	£20.00

LEWIS & ALLEN CO. U.S.A.

	L	250	Views & Art Studies (1910–15)	£1.50	—

LONE JACK CIGARETTE CO., U.S.A.

		50	Language of Flowers (1885–92)	£10.00	—

P. LORILLARD CO., U.S.A.

Issues 1885–98

	Size			Price	
	M	25	Actresses RB23/L70–4–3.................................	£7.50	—
	M	25	Actresses RB23/L70–5..................................	£6.00	—
	EL	25	Actresses RB23/L70–6:—		
			A. "Red Cross" Long Cut..............................	£6.00	—
			B. "Sensation Cut Plug" Front & Back	£6.00	—
			C. "Sensation Cut Plug" Front Only....................	£6.00	—
	EL	25	Actresses RB23/L70–8	£7.50	—
	EL	25	Actresses in Opera Roles RB23/L70–9	£12.50	—
	M	25	Ancient Mythology Burlesqued RB23/L70–10	£5.00	—
	M	50	Beautiful Women RB23/L70–11:—		
			A. "5c Ante" Front & Back	£6.00	—
			B. "Lorillard's Snuff" Front & Back.....................	£8.00	—
			C. "Tiger" Front & Back..............................	£8.00	—
	EL	25	Circus Scenes..	£15.00	—
	EL	50	Prizefighters..	£15.00	—
	M	25	Types of the Stage	£7.50	—

W. C. MACDONALD INC., Canada

Illus. No.	Size	Number in set		Price per card	Complete set
194		?	Aeroplane & Warships (1926–47)..........................	40p	—
	M	53	Playing Cards (Different Designs) (1926–47)	25p	—

B. & J. B. MACHADO, Jamaica

Illus. No.	Size	Number in set		Price per card	Complete set
		25	British Naval Series (1916)	£5.00	—
		50	The Great War – Victoria Cross Heroes (1916–17)...........	£6.00	—
	P	50	Popular Film Stars (1926)	—	—
	P	50	The Royal Family at Home & Abroad (1927)	—	—
	P	52	Stars of the Cinema (1926)	—	—
	P	50	The World of Sport (1928)	—	—

MACLIN – ZIMMER – MCGILL TOB. CO. U.S.A.

	EL	53	Playing Cards – Actresses (1885–95)	£6.00	—

H. MANDELBAUM U.S.A.

		20	Types of People (1888–92)................................	£15.00	—

MARBURG BROS., U.S.A.

		48	National Costume Cards (1885–91)........................	—	—

P. H. MAYO & BROTHER, U.S.A.

Illus. No.	Size	Number in set		Price per card	Complete set
		25	Actresses RB23/M80–1	£6.00	—
	M	25	Actresses RB23/M80–3	£10.00	—
	L	12	Actresses RB23/M80–4	£20.00	—
		?39	Actresses RB23/M80–5	£12.50	—
		40	Baseball Players	£20.00	—
		20	Costumes & Flowers......................................	£7.50	—
		25	Head Dresses of Various Nations..........................	£10.00	—
	M	25	National Flowers (Girl & Scene)..........................	£10.00	—
150		20	Naval Uniforms	£10.00	—
		35	Prizefighters..	£7.50	—
		20	Shakespeare Characters..................................	£10.00	—

M. MELACHRINO & CO., Switzerland

		52	Peuples Exotiques (1920–30) 1st Series	20p	£10.00
		52	Peuples Exotiques (1920–30) 2nd Series	20p	£10.00
		52	Peuples Exotiques (1920–30) 3rd Series	20p	£10.00

MIFSUF & AZZOPARDI, Malta

	KP	59	First Maltese Parliament (1922)	£3.00	—

L. MILLER & SONS, U.S.A.

89	M	25	Battleships (1895–1905)...................................	£7.50	—
	M	25	Generals & Admirals (Spanish War) (1895–1905)............	£5.00	—
	M	24	Presidents of U.S. (1895–1905)...........................	£5.00	—
	L	50	Rulers of the World (1895–1905)	£5.00	—

CHAS. J. MITCHELL & CO., Canada

		26	Actresses, "FROGA A" (1900–05):—		
			A. Backs in Brown....................................	£10.00	—
			B. Backs in Green	£10.00	—

MITSUI & CO., Japan

87		?	Japanese Women (1905–10)	£1.00	—

MOORE & CALVI, U.S.A.

	EL	53	Playing Cards – Actresses (1885–95):—		
			A. "Trumps Long Cut" Back...........................	£8.00	—
			B. "Hard-A-Port" with Makers Name...................	£6.00	—
			C. "Hard-A-Port" without Makers Name................	£6.00	—

MURAI BROS. & CO., Japan

		150	Actresses "ALWICS" (Pre 1918)	60p	—
		100	Beauties "THIBS".......................................	£3.00	—
		50	Beauties Group 1	£6.00	—
		50	Chinese Girls...	£3.00	—
		25	Chinese Beauties 1st Series Peacock Issue	80p	£20.00
		25	Chinese Beauties 3rd Series Peacock Issue....................	£1.00	—
		50	Chinese Childrens Games without Border Peacock Issue......	£1.00	—

MURAI BROS. & CO., Japan *(continued)*

Illus. No.	Size	Number in set		Price per card	Complete set
92		20	Chinese Childrens Games with Border Peacock Issue	£1.00	—
		100	Chinese, Korean or Japanese Girls	£2.00	—
		50	Chinese Pagodas Peacock Issue......................	80p	—
		30	Chinese Series Peacock Issue	£1.00	—
		50	Dancing Girls of the World	£8.00	—

NATIONAL CIGARETTE AND TOBACCO CO., U.S.A. ───────

Issued 1888–1905

Illus. No.	Size	Number in set		Price per card	Complete set
	EL	13	Art Miniatures	£17.50	—
	EL	?	Cabinet Pictures	£17.50	—
155		25	National Types	£6.00	£150.00
		44	National Types	£8.00	—

Photographic Cards

		?	Actresses:—		
			A. Plain Back	£1.25	—
			B. Printed Back	£3.00	—

OGDENS LIMITED ──────────────────────

Illus. No.	Size	Number in set		Price per card	Complete set
		51	Actresses Black & White Polo Issue (1906–08)...............	£2.00	—
93		30	Actresses Unicoloured Polo Issue (1908):—		
			A. Tin Foil at back white....................	80p	£24.00
			B. Tin Foil at back shaded	£1.00	£30.00
		17	Animals Polo Issue (1916)	£6.00	—
		60	Animals—Cut Outs:—		
			A. Ruler Issue (1912)......................	£1.00	—
			B. Tabs Issue (1913):—		
			i) with captions	80p	—
			ii) without captions......................	£2.00	—
		50	Aviation Series Tabs Issue (1912):—		
			A. Ogdens at base......................	£1.25	—
			B. Ogdens England at base	£1.50	—
		?98	Beauties Green Net Design Back (1901)......................	£5.00	—
		45	Beauties Picture Hats Polo Issue (1911)	£2.00	—
		50	Best Dogs of their Breed Polo Issue (1916):—		
			A. Back in Red	£3.00	—
			B. Back in Blue......................	£2.50	—
132		52	Birds of Brilliant Plumage Ruler Issue (1914):—		
			A. Fronts with Framelines	80p	£40.00
			B. Fronts without Framelines	80p	—
84		25	British Trees & Their Uses Guinea Gold Issue (1927)	80p	£20.00
		25	China's Famous Warriors Ruler Issue (1913)...............	£2.00	—
		25	Famous Railway Trains Guinea Gold issue (1928)............	£1.00	£25.00
		20	Flower's Polo Issue (1915):—		
			A. Without Eastern Inscription......................	£3.00	—
			B. With Eastern Inscription	£3.00	—
		25	Indian Women Polo Issue (1919):—		
			A. Framework in Apple Green	£1.50	—
			B. Framework in Emerald Green	£1.75	—
	K	52	Miniature Playing Cards Polo Issue (1922)......................	—	—
		50	Music Hall Celebrities (1911):—		
			A. Polo Issue	£1.50	—
			B. Tabs Issue......................	£1.50	—
83		50	Riders of the World Polo Issue (1911)......................	£1.00	£50.00
		50	Russo-Japanese Series (1905)......................	—	—
		36	Ships & Their Pennants Polo Issue (1911)	£2.00	—
		32	Transport of the World Polo Issue (1917)	£2.00	—

OLD FASHION, U.S.A. ──────────────────

Illus. No.	Size	Number in set		Price per card	Complete set
	L	?	Photographic Cards	£2.00	—

PENINSULAR TOBACCO CO. LTD., India ──────────

Illus. No.	Size	Number in set		Price per card	Complete set
		50	Animals & Birds (1910)	£1.00	—
		52	Birds of Brilliant Plumage (1916):—		
			A. Back with single large packings	—	—
			B. Back with two small packings......................	—	—
		25	Birds of the East 1st series (1912)	80p	—
91		25	Birds of the East 2nd Series (1912)	50p	£12.50
		25	Chinese Famous Warriors:—		
			A. Back "Monchyr India"	£1.00	£25.00
			B. Back "India" only	80p	£20.00
		50	Chinese Heroes (1913)	£1.00	—
		50	Chinese Modern Beauties (1912)......................	£2.00	—
		50	Chinese Trades (1908):—		
			A. Back with "Monchyr"	—	—
			B. Back without "Monchyr"	—	—
		30	Fish Series (1916)	—	—
		25	Hindoo Gods (1909)	80p	£20.00
		37	Nautch Girl Series (1910–12)	£2.00	—
		25	Products of the World (1915)......................	80p	—

PLANTERS' STORES & AGENCY CO. LTD., India

Illus. No.	Size	Number in set		Price per card	Complete set
122		?47	Actresses "FROGA" (1900–03)	£10.00	—
		25	Beauties "FECKSA" (1900–03)	£10.00	—

JOHN PLAYER & SONS

A. Channel Islands Issues (without I.T.C. Clause)

Illus. No.	Size	Number in set		Price per card	Complete set
186		50	Aircraft of the Royal Air Force (1938)	30p	£15.00
		50	Animals of the Countryside (1939)	25p	£12.50
		50	Birds & Their Young (1937)	20p	£10.00
176		50	Coronation Series Ceremonial Dress (1937)	20p	£10.00
192		50	Cricketers (1938)	30p	£15.00
		50	Cycling (1939)	25p	£12.50
	L	25	Famous Beauties (1937)	60p	£15.00
		50	Film Stars 3rd Series (1938)	30p	£15.00
	L	25	Golf (1929)	20p	£5.00
		50	International Air Liners (1936)	20p	£10.00
193		50	Military Uniforms of the British Empire Overseas (1938):—		
			A. Adhesive Backs	30p	£15.00
			B. Non-Adhesive Backs	30p	£15.00
		50	Modern Naval Craft (1939)	25p	£12.50
		50	Motor Cars 1st Series (1936)	40p	£20.00
		50	Motor Cars 2nd Series (1937)	40p	£20.00
177		50	National Flags & Arms (1936)	20p	£10.00
	L	25	Old Hunting Prints (1938)	80p	—
	L	25	Old Naval Prints (1936)	80p	£20.00
	L	25	Racing Yachts (1938)	80p	—
		50	R.A.F. Badges (1937)	20p	£10.00
190		50	Sea Fishes (1935)	20p	£10.00
	L	25	Types of Horses (1939)	80p	£20.00
	L	25	Zoo Babies (1937)	80p	—

B. General Overseas Issues

Illus. No.	Size	Number in set		Price per card	Complete set
		50	Aeroplane Series (1926)	70p	—
		50	Arms & Armour (1926)	£1.00	£50.00
	MP	50	Beauties 1st Series (1925):—		
			A. Black & White Fronts	50p	£25.00
			B. Coloured Fronts	70p	£35.00
	MP	50	Beauties 2nd Series (1925)	60p	£30.00
		52	Birds of Brilliant Plumage (1927)	£1.25	—
		25	Bonzo Dogs (1923)	£1.00	£25.00
		50	Boy Scouts (1924)	£1.00	—
	M	25	British Live Stock (1924)	£1.00	—
		50	Butterflies (Girls) (1928)	£1.25	—
86		25	Dogs (Heads) (1927)	30p	£7.50
		32	Drum Horses (1911)	£3.00	—
90		25	Flag Girls of All Nations (1908)	£2.50	—
		50	Household Hints (1928–29)	80p	—
		50	Lawn Tennis (1928)	£1.00	—
		50	Leaders of Men (1925)	80p	£40.00
		48	Pictures of the East (1931)	£1.00	£50.00
		25	Picturesque People of the Empire (1928)	£1.00	£25.00
	M	53	Playing Cards (1929)	80p	—
104		50	Pugilists in Action (1928)	£1.00	—
98		50	Railway Working (1926)	80p	£40.00
	P	50	The Royal Family at Home & Abroad (1927)	£1.00	—
		50	Ships, Flags & Cap badges (1930)	80p	£40.00
		50	Signalling Series (1926)	80p	—
88		25	Whaling (1930)	80p	£20.00

POLICANSKY BROS., South Africa

Illus. No.	Size	Number in set		Price per card	Complete set
		50	Beautiful Illustrations of South African Fauna (1925)	£4.00	—

RICHMOND CAVENDISH CO. LTD.

Illus. No.	Size	Number in set		Price per card	Complete set
		28	Chinese Actors & Actresses (1922)	£1.25	—
	P	50	Cinema Stars (1926)	80p	—

RUGGIER BROS. Malta

Illus. No.	Size	Number in set		Price per card	Complete set
	M	50	Story of the Knights of Malta (1920–30)	£1.00	—

SCERRI, Malta

Illus. No.	Size	Number in set		Price per card	Complete set
156			**Beauties & Children (1920–40)**		
		150	A. Black & White, No Borders	30p	—
		?86	B. Black & White, White Border	£1.00	—
		45	C. Coloured	40p	£18.00
	MP	50	Beautiful Women (1920–40)	60p	£30.00
	MP	480	Cinema Artists (1920–40)	50p	—
	MP	180	Cinema Stars (1920–40)	50p	—
	MP	50	Famous London Buildings (1920–40)	£1.00	£50.00
	MP	60	Film Stars 1st Series No. 1–60	50p	—
	MP	60	Film Stars 2nd Series No. 61–120	50p	—

Illus. No.	Size	Number in set		Price per card	Complete set
		52	Interesting Places of the World (1920–40)	25p	£12.50
	P	25	International Footballers (1920–40)	—	—
141	M	401	Malta Views (1920–40).......................................	25p	—
153	M	51	Members of Parliament – Malta (1920–40)	15p	£7.50
99		146	Prominent People (1920–40).................................	50p	—
	MP	100	Scenes from Films (1920–40)	50p	—
	LP	100	Talkie Stars (1920–40)	70p	—
	M	100	Worlds Famous People (1920–40)	25p	£25.00

J. J. SCHUH TOBACCO CO. PTY. LTD., Australia ─────────────

Issues 1920–25

		60	Australian Footballers Series A (half-full length)	£3.00	—
		40	Australian Footballers Series B (Rays).......................	£2.00	—
		59	Australian Footballers Series C (Oval Frame)	£3.00	—
			Australian Jockeys:—		
		30	A. Numbered..	—	—
		30	B. Unnumbered	—	—
	P	72	Cinema Stars	£1.00	—
		60	Cinema Stars	—	—
	L	12	Maxims of Success..	—	—
	P	72	Official War Photographs	£2.00	—
	P	96	Portraits of Our Leading Footballers	£2.00	—

G. SCLIVAGNOTTI, Malta ───────────────────────

181		50	Actresses & Cinema Stars (1923–24)	50p	£25.00
	MP	71	Grand Masters of the Orders of Jerusalem (1897–99)	—	—
	P	102	Opera Singers (1897–99)	—	—
	M	102	Opera Singers (1897–99)	—	—

SIMONETS LTD., Jersey, Channel Islands ───────────

	MP	36	Beautiful Women (1920–30).................................	£1.25	—
	P	24	Cinema Scenes Series (1920–30)	80p	£20.00
	P	27	Famous Actors & Actresses (1920–30)	80p	£22.00
		50	Local Footballers (1913–14).................................	£1.25	—
189	P	27	Sporting Celebrities (1920–30)..............................	£1.00	£27.00

THE SINSOCK & CO., Korea ──────────────────────

		20	Korean Girls (1900–05)	£5.00	—

SNIDERS & ABRAHAMS PTY. LTD., Australia ─────────

Issues 1904–1920

		30	Actresses Gold Background...............................	£5.00	—
		20	Actresses White Borders	£5.00	—
		20	Admirals and Warships of USA	£5.00	—
		60	Animals..	£1.00	—
199		60	Animals and Birds:—		
			A. "Advertisement Gifts" issue......................	80p	—
			B. "Peter Pan" issue	£1.00	£60.00
		15	Australian Cricket Team (1905)	—	—
		16	Australian Football Incidents in Play	£4.00	—
		24	Australian Footballers (Full Length) Series A1 with Blue Framelines..	£6.00	—
		50	Australian Footballers (Full Length) Series AII without Framelines...	£6.00	—
		76	Australian Footballers (½ length) Series B	£5.00	—
		76	Australian Footballers (½ length) Series C	£4.00	—
		140	Australian Footballers (Head & Shoulders) Series D.........	£4.00	—
		60	Australian Footballers (Head in Oval) Series E..............	£4.00	—
		60	Australian Footballers (Head in Rays) Series F.............	£4.00	—
		60	Australian Footballers (with Pennant) Series G	£4.00	—
		60	Australian Footballers (Head in Star) Series H	£4.00	—
		60	Australian Footballers (Head in Shield) Series I	£4.00	—
		56	Australian Footballers (½–¾ length) Series J.............	—	—
		48	Australian Jockeys Back in Blue..........................	£2.00	—
		83	Australian Jockeys Back in Brown........................	£2.00	—
149		56	Australian Racehorses Horizontal Back	£2.00	—
		56	Australian Racehorses Vertical Back	£2.00	—
		40	Australian Racing Scenes	£2.00	—
		132	Australian VC's and Officers	£2.50	—
		12	Billiard Tricks	£3.00	—
		60	Butterflies & Moths Captions in small letters	£1.00	—
		60	Butterflies & Moths Captions in block letters.............	£1.00	—
		60	Cartoons & Caricatures..................................	£4.00	—
		12	Coin Tricks	£3.00	—
152		64	Crests of British Warships...............................	£2.00	—
		40	Cricketers in Action	£6.00	—

SNIDERS & ABRAHAMS PTY. LTD., Australia *(continued)*

Illus. No.	Size	Number in set		Price per card	Complete set
		12	Cricket Terms	£5.00	—
		32	Dickens Series	£2.00	—
		16	Dogs:—		
			A. "Standard" issue	£2.50	—
			B. "Peter Pan" issue:—		
			1. White Panel	£3.50	—
			2. Gilt Panel	£3.00	—
			C. "Coronet" Issue	£3.00	—
		6	Flags (Shaped Metal)	£2.00	—
		6	Flags (Shaped Card)	£2.00	—
		60	Great War Leaders & Warships:—		
			A. Front in Green	£2.00	—
			B. Front in Sepia Brown	£2.00	—
151		30	How to Keep Fit	£3.00	—
		60	Jokes:—		
			A. "Aristocratica" issue	£3.00	—
			B. "Standard" issue	£2.00	—
		12	Match Puzzles	£3.00	—
		48	Medals & Decorations	£3.00	—
	M	48	Melbourne Buildings	£5.00	—
		25	Natives of the World	£5.00	—
		12	Naval Terms	£3.00	—
		29	Oscar Asche, Lily Brayton & Lady Smokers	£4.00	—
		40	Shakespeare Characters	£3.00	—
		30	Signalling – Semaphore & Morse	—	—
		14	Statuary	—	—
		60	Street Criers in London (1907)	—	—
		32	Views of Victoria in 1857	—	—
	P	174	Views of the World	£1.50	—

STAR TOBACCO CO., India

| | | 52 | Beauties (P/C inset) (1895–1905) . . . . | — | — |
| | | 52 | Indian Native Types (P/C inset) (1895–1905) . . . . | — | — |

TEOFANI & CO. LTD.

| | MP | 50 | Teofani's Icelandic Employees (1930) . . . . | £1.50 | — |

TOBACCO PRODUCTS CORPORATION U.S.A.

| | | 220 | Movie Stars (1915) . . . . | 80p | — |

TOBACCO PRODUCTS CORPORATION OF CANADA LTD.

		?45	Canadian Sports Champions (1920's)	—	—
		60	Do You Know (1924)	£2.50	—
		60	Hockey Players (1926)	£3.00	—
		120	Movie Stars (1920's)	£1.75	—
		?163	Movie Stars Set 4 (1920's)	£1.75	—

TUCKETT LIMITED, Canada

		25	Autograph Series (1910–15)	£10.00	—
		160	Beauties & Scenes (1910–15)	£5.00	—
		25	Boy Scout Series (1910–15)	—	—
	P	100	British Views without Tucketts on front (1910–15)	80p	—
	P	?218	British Views with Tucketts on front (1910–15)	£1.00	—
105	P	80	British Warships (1910–15)	£2.00	—
	P	50	Canadian Scenes (1910–15)	80p	—
		53	Playing Card Premium Certificates (1923–31)	£2.00	—
		52	Tucketts Aeroplane Series (1930)	£2.00	—
		52	Tucketts Aviation Series (1929)	£2.00	—
		52	Tucketts Auction Bridge Series (1923–31)	£2.00	—

UNITED TOBACCO COMPANIES (SOUTH) LTD., South Africa

A. With Firms Name

117		50	Aeroplanes of Today (1936):—		
			A. "Box 78 Capetown"	50p	£25.00
			B. "Box 1006 Capetown"	50p	£25.00
		50	Animals & Birds Koodoo Issue (1920–25)	£1.50	—
	L	24	Arms & Crests of Universities & Schools of South Africa (1930)	40p	£10.00
154	L	52	Boy Scouts, Girl Guide & Voortrekker Badges (1932)	40p	£20.00
	L	62	British Rugby Tour of South Africa (1938)	30p	£20.00
		50	Children of All Nations (1928)	50p	—
		50	Cinema Stars "Flag Cigarettes" (1924)	50p	£25.00
		60	Do You Know? (1929)	30p	£18.00
		50	Do You Know 2nd Series (1930)	30p	£15.00
		50	Do You Know 3rd Series (1931)	30p	£15.00
	K	28	Dominoes "Ruger Cigarettes" (1934)	—	—
	L	50	Exercises for Men & Women (1932)	30p	£15.00

Illus. No.	Size	Number in set		Price per card	Complete set
		48	Fairy Tales 1st Series Flag Issue (1928)	60p	—
		48	Fairy Tales 2nd Series Flag Issue (1928)	60p	—
		24	Fairy Tales (1926) (Booklets)	—	—
	L	120	Farmyards of South Africa (1934)	20p	£24.00
	M	50	Household Tips (1926)	—	—
118		25	Interesting Experiments (1930)	40p	£10.00
158	L	100	Medals & Decorations of the British commonwealth of Nations (1941)	25p	—
		50	Merchant Ships of the World (1925)	50p	£25.00
		50	Motor Cars (1923)	£1.50	—
	L	100	Our Land (1938)	13p	£10.00
157	L	200	Our South Africa Past & Present (1938)	13p	£15.00
	L	24	Pastel Plates (1938)	40p	£10.00
	L	88	Philosophical Sayings (1938)	60p	—
119		25	Picturesque People of the Empire (1929)	40p	£10.00
	K	53	Playing Cards "Flag" Cigarettes	£1.00	—
	K	53	Playing Cards "Lifeboat" Cigarettes (1934)	75p	—
	M	53	Playing Cards "Lotus Cigarettes" (1934–35)	—	—
	L	53	Playing Cards "Loyalist Cigarettes" (1934–35)	—	—
	K	53	Playing Cards "MP Cigarettes" (1934–35)	—	—
	K	53	Playing Cards "Ruger Cigarettes" (1934–35)	—	—
	L	50	Racehorses South Africa Set 1 (1929)	50p	—
	L	52	Racehorses South Africa Set 2 (1930):—		
			A. Inscribed "a series of 50"	50p	—
			B. Inscribed "a series of 52"	40p	—
121		50	Regimental Uniforms (1937)	60p	£30.00
120		50	Riders of the World (1931)	50p	£25.00
		25	South African Birds 1st Series (1927)	80p	—
		25	South African Birds 2nd Series (1927)	80p	—
112	L	52	South African Butterflies (1937)	25p	£12.50
113	L	52	South African Coats of Arms (1931)	20p	£10.00
	L	52	South African Flora (1935):—		
			A. With "CT Ltd"	40p	—
			B. Without "CT Ltd"	20p	£10.00
	L	65	South African Rugby Football Clubs (1933)	30p	£20.00
	L	52	Sports & Pastimes of South Africa (1936)	30p	£15.00
109	L	47	Springbok Rugby and Cricket Teams (1931)	50p	—
	L	28	1912–13 Sprinkboks (1913)	—	—
		25	Studdy Dogs (1925)	£1.50	—
	L	40	Views of South African Scenery 1st Series (1918):—		
			A. Text Back	£1.25	—
			B. Anonymous Plain Back	£1.50	—
	L	36	Views of South African Scenery 2nd Series (1920)	£1.25	—
		25	Wild Flowers of South Africa 1st Series (1925)	80p	—
		25	Wild Flowers of South Africa 2nd Series (1926)	80p	—
		50	The World of Tomorrow (1938)	20p	£10.00

B. Without Firms Name

Illus. No.	Size	Number in set		Price per card	Complete set
140		50	African Fish (1937)	50p	£25.00
		50	British Aeroplanes (1933)	80p	—
	EL	25	Champion Dogs (1934)	£1.00	—
		30	Do You Know (1933)	40p	£12.00
		50	Eminent Film Personalities (1930)	80p	—
17		50	English Period Costumes (1932)	30p	£15.00
		25	Famous Figures from South African History (1932)	£1.00	—
	L	100	Famous Works of Art (1939)	13p	£10.00
		25	Flowers of Africa (1932)	80p	—
	M	50	Humour in Sport (1929)	80p	—
	L	100	Our Land (1938)	20p	—
110	M	150	Our South African Birds (1942)	13p	£15.00
	L	150	Our South African Birds (1942)	13p	£15.00
111	M	100	Our South African Flora (1940)	13p	£10.00
	L	100	Our South African Flora (1940)	13p	£10.00
	M	100	Our South African National Parks (1941)	13p	£10.00
	L	100	Our South African National Parks (1941)	13p	£10.00
	L	50	Pictures of South Africa War Effort (1942)	20p	£10.00
		50	Riders of the World (1931)	60p	£30.00
		50	Safety First (1936)	30p	£15.00
115	M	40	Ships of All Times (1931)	60p	—
		25	South African Birds 2nd Series	£1.50	—
	L	17	South African Cricket Touring Team (1929):—		
			A. Fronts with Autographs	—	—
			B. Fronts without Autographs	—	—
148	M	100	South African Defence (1939)	13p	£10.00
	L	50	South African Places of Interest (1934)	20p	£10.00
	P	50	Stereoscopic Photographs Assorted Subjects (1928)	80p	—
	P	50	Stereoscopic Photographs of South Africa (1929)	80p	—
114		50	The Story of Sand (1934)	30.	£15.00
	M	50	Tavern of the Seas (1939)	15p	£7.50
144		25	Warriors of the World (Crossed Swords at Base) (1937)	60p	£15.00
		25	What's This (1929)	£1.00	£25.00
116		50	Wild Animals of the World (1932)	40p	£20.00
	M	40	Wonders of the World (1931)	50p	—
	M	100	World Famous Boxers (1930–35)	50p	—

C. Silks Issues 1910–17

Illus. No.	Size	Number in set		Price per card	Complete set
	M	20	British Butterflies	—	—
	M	30	British Roses	—	—
	M	65	Flags of All Nations	£1.50	—

Illus. No.	Size	Number in set		Price per card	Complete set
	M	25	Old Masters...	£4.00	—
	M	50	Pottery Types (1918–43).............................	£3.00	—
	M	50	South African Flowers Nd 1–50......................	£1.50	—
	M	50	South African Flowers Nd 51–100...................	£1.50	—

UNIVERSAL TOBACCO CO. PTY. LTD, South Africa _____

		835	Flags of All Nations (1935)...........................	50p	—

S. W. VENABLE TOBACCO CO., U.S.A. _____

	EL	?	Actresses..	£7.50	—

WESTMINSTER TOBACCO CO. LTD. _____

A. Card Issues

Illus. No.	Size	Number in set		Price per card	Complete set
	M	332	Adamsons Oplevelser (1930)............................	—	—
	M	50	Beauties (1924)......................................	60p	—
	MP	100	Beautiful Women (1915)...............................	60p	—
	M	50	Birds, Beasts & Fishes (1923).........................	80p	—
	M	102	British Beauties (coloured) (1915).....................	£1.00	—
	M	102	British Beauties (uncoloured) (1915)...................	—	—
	P	48	British Royal & Ancient Buildings (1925)...............	40p	£20.00
	M	50	Butterflies & Moths (1920)............................	£1.00	—
	P	36	Canada 1st Series (1926).............................	40p	£15.00
	P	36	Canada 2nd Series (1928)............................	40p	£15.00
182		30	Celebrated Actresses (1921)..........................	£1.25	—
		100	Cinema Artistes Green Back (1929–33).................	—	—
		50	Cinema Artistes Grey Back (1929–33)..................	—	—
		48	Cinema Celebrities (1935)............................	—	—
	P	50	Cinema Stars (1926).................................	£1.00	—
	MP	50	Cinema Stars (1930).................................	£1.00	—
	M	27	Dancing Girls (1917)................................	£1.00	—
		50	Do You Know (1922).................................	80p	—
		24	Fairy Tale (Booklets) (1926)..........................	—	—
	M	100	Famous Beauties (1916):—		
			A. Captions in Brown...............................	75p	—
			B. Captions in Blue................................	75p	—
	MP	52	Film Favourites (1927):—		
			A. Uncoloured	80p	—
			B. Coloured......................................	80p	—
	M	50	Film Personalities (1931).............................	£1.00	—
82	M	50	Garden Flowers of the World (1917)....................	80p	—
		40	The Great War Celebrities (1914)......................	£2.50	—
	P	48	Indian Empire 1st Series (1925).......................	40p	£20.00
	P	48	Indian Empire 2nd Series (1926)......................	40p	£20.00
	LP	50	Islenzkar Eimskipamyndir (1931)......................	80p	—
	LP	50	Islenzkar Landslagmyndir (1928)......................	80p	—
	LP	50	Islenzkar Landslagmyndir 2nd Series (1929)............	80p	—
		40	Merrie England Studies (1914)........................	£1.50	—
		36	Modern Beauties (1938)..............................	£1.75	—
	MP	52	Movie Stars (1925)..................................	60p	—
	P	36	New Zealand 1st Series (1928)........................	40p	£15.00
	P	36	New Zealand 2nd Series (1929).......................	40p	£15.00
	K	53	Playing Cards (1934)................................	50p	—
	M	55	Playing Cards (1934):—		
			A. Blue Back......................................	50p	—
			B. Red Back......................................	50p	—
	P	50	Popular Film Stars (1926)............................	70p	—
	P	36	South Africa 1st Series (1928)........................	40p	£15.00
	P	36	South Africa 2nd Series (1928).......................	40p	£15.00
81	M	49	South African Succulents (1936)......................	13p	£5.00
	M	100	Stage & Cinema Stars Captions in Grey (1921).........	60p	—
	M	100	Stage & Cinema Stars Captions in Black (1921)........	50p	—
	M	50	Stars of Filmland (1927).............................	£1.00	—
		50	Steamships of the World (1920).......................	£2.50	—
	M	50	Uniforms of All Ages (1917)..........................	£3.00	—
	P	50	Views of Malaya (1930)..............................	£2.50	—
		25	Wireless (1923)	80p	—
	M	49	Women of All Nations (1922).........................	£1.00	—
85		50	The World of Tomorrow (1938)........................	20p	£10.00

B. Silk Issues

	M	50	Garden Flowers of the World (1914–18).................	£1.50	—
	M	?	Miniature Rugs.....................................	£5.00	—

W. D. & H. O. WILLS _____

A. Channel Island Issues (without I.T.C. Clause)

Illus. No.		Number in set		Price per card	Complete set
		50	Air Raid Precautions	20p	£10.00
		50	Association Footballers (1936)........................	20p	£10.00
		50	Dogs (1937)..	20p	£10.00
		50	Garden Flowers by Richard Sudell (1939)..............	20p	£10.00
		50	Garden Hints (1938).................................	20p	£10.00
191		50	Household Hints (1936)..............................	20p	£10.00

Illus. No.	Size	Number in set		Price per card	Complete set
		50	Life in the Royal Navy (1939)	13p	£5.00
		50	Our King & Queen (1937)	20p	£10.00
		50	Railway Equipment (1939)	20p	£10.00
		50	The Sea Shore (1938)	20p	£10.00
185		50	Speed (1938)	20p	£10.00
		50	Wild Flowers 1st Series (1936)	20p	£10.00
		50	Wild Flowers 2nd Series (1937)	20p	£10.00

B. General Overseas Issues

Illus. No.	Size	Number in set		Price per card	Complete set
		50	Actors & Actresses Scroll Backs in Green (1903–10) Ref. 32		
			A. Portraits in Black & White	—	—
			B. Portraits Flesh Tinted	80p	—
		30	Actresses – Brown & Green (1905–10) Ref. 116 Scissors Issue	£1.50	£45.00
		50	Actresses – Four Colours Surround (1903–08) Ref. 117:—		
			A. Scissors Issue	£2.00	—
			B. Green Scroll Back Issue	60p	—
		30	Actresses – Orange/Mauve Surround (1910–15) Scissors Issue Ref. 118:—		
			A. Surround in Orange	80p	£24.00
			B. Surround in Mauve	60p	£18.00
		100	Actresses (1903–10) Ref. 34:—		
			A. Capstan Issue	£1.20	—
			B. Vice Regal Issue	£1.20	—
		250	Actresses (1903–10) Ref. 33:—		
			A. Front Portrait in Black	60p	—
			B. Front Portrait in Red	—	—
		25	Actresses – Tabs Type Numbered Ref. 16	£4.00	—
		50	Actresses – Tabs Type Unnumbered Ref. 119 Scissors Issue	£5.00	—
		30	Actresses Unicoloured 1 (1908–13) Ref. 120:—		
			A. Scissors Issue Back in Red	60p	£18.00
			B. Scissors Issue Back in Purple Brown	80p	£24.00
		30	Actresses – Unicoloured 11 (1908–13) Ref. 121 Scissors Issue	60p	£18.00
		50	Aeroplanes (1925)	80p	—
		60	Animals (Cut-Outs) (1910–15):—		
			A. Havelock Issue	30p	£18.00
			B. Wills Specialities Issue	30p	£18.00
		50	Animals & Birds (1910):—		
			A. With Text, Without Title	80p	—
			B. Without Text, With Title (1912)	80p	—
			C. Without Text or Title	80p	—
123		50	Arms & Armour (1910):—		
			A. Capstan Issue	70p	—
			B. Havelock Issue	—	—
			C. Vice Regal Issue	70p	—
			D. United Service Issue	80p	£40.00
196		50	Arms of the British Empire (1910):—		
			A. Backs in Black	40p	£20.00
			B. Wills Specialities Issue	60p	—
			C. Havelock Issue	£5.00	—
201		25	Army Life 1910 Scissors Issue	80p	£20.00
		50	Art Photogravures 1st Series (1913–14):—		
			A. Size 67 × 33 mm.	40p	—
			B. Size 67 × 44 mm.	40p	—
		50	Art Photogravures 2nd Series (1913–14)	40p	—
		42	Australian Club Cricketers (1905) Ref. 59A:—		
			A. Dark Blue Backs	£5.00	—
			B. Green Backs	£5.00	—
			C. Pale Blue Backs	£6.00	—
		25	Australian and English Cricketers (1903) Ref. 59B	£4.00	—
		25	Australian and English Cricketers (1909) Ref. 59C:—		
			A. Capstan Issue:—		
			i) Framework in Scarlet	£5.00	—
			ii) Framework in Blue	£5.00	—
			B. Vice Regal Issue:—		
			i) Framework in Scarlet	£5.00	—
			ii) Framework in Blue	£5.00	—
		60	Australian and South African Cricketers (1910–11) Ref. 59D:—		
			A. Capstan Issue:—		
			i) Framework in Scarlet	£5.00	—
			ii) Framework in Blue	£5.00	—
			B. Havelock Issue:—		
			i) Framework in Scarlet	—	—
			ii) Framework in Blue	—	—
			C. Vice Regal Issue:—		
			i) Framework in Scarlet	£5.00	—
			ii) Framework in Blue	£5.00	—
	M	100	Australian Scenic Series (1928)	50p	—
		50	Australian Wild Flowers (1913):—		
			A. Will's Specialities Issue Grey-Brown Back	40p	£20.00
			B. Will's Specialities Issue Green Back	—	—
			C. Havelock Issue	£3.00	—
147			Aviation (1910):—		
		85	A. Black Backs "Series of 85":—		
			i) Capstan Issue	90p	
			ii) Vice Regal issue	90p	—
		75	B. Black Backs "Series of 75":—		
			i) Capstan Issue	60p	—
			ii) Havelock Issue	£1.25	—

Illus. No.	Size	Number in set		Price per card	Complete set
			iii) Vice Regal issue	60p	—
		75	C. Green Back "Series of 75":—		
			i) Capstan Issue	80p	—
			ii) Havelock Issue	£3.00	—
			iii) Vice Regal issue	80p	—
		50	Aviation Series (1910–11):—		
			A. W. D. & H. D. Wills Back	80p	—
			B. Anonymous Backs with Album Clause	90p	—
			C. Anonymous Backs without Album Clause	£1.00	—
		?95	Baseball Series (1912) Private Issue	£10.00	—
		40	Beauties – Brown Tinted (1910–15):—		
			A. Scissors Issue	50p	£20.00
			B. Star Circle and Leaves issue	80p	—
		30	Beauties – "Celebrated Actresses" Ref. 140 Scissors Issue	£2.00	—
125		52	Beauties – Heads and Shoulders Set in Background Ref. 141:—		
			A. Scissors Issue:—		
			i) Background to Packets Plain	90p	—
			ii) Background to Packets Latticework Design	80p	£40.00
			B. Star Circle and Leaves Issue	£1.25	
	P	25	Beauties 1st Series (1924–25) Ref. 142	£1.00	—
	P	50	Beauties 2nd Series (1924–25) Ref. 143	£1.00	—
		32	Beauties – Picture Hats (1910–15) Ref. 144:—		
			A. Scissors Issue	£1.00	£32.00
			B. Star Circle and Leaves Issue	£1.00	—
	MP	72	Beauties – Red Star and Circle Back (1910–15) Ref. 145	£3.00	—
		50	Beauties – Red Tinted (1905–10) Ref. 146	60p	£30.00
		30	Beauties and Children (1910–15) Ref. 147 Scissors Issue	£1.00	£30.00
124	P	50	Beautiful New Zealand (1925–30)	20p	£10.00
		50	Best Dogs of Their Breed (1916):—		
			A. Havelock Issue	£2.00	—
			B. Will's Specialities Issue	70p	—
			C. Anonymous Back, Will's on Front	£3.00	—
		30	Birds and Animals (1911) Ruby Queen Issue	£1.00	—
		50	Birds, Beasts & Fishes (1925–30)	20p	£10.00
		100	Birds of Australasia (1912):—		
			A. Green Backs:—		
			i) Capstan Issue	35p	£35.00
			ii) Havelock Issue	80p	—
			iii) Vice Regal Issue	35p	£35.00
			B. Yellow Backs:—		
			i) Havelock Issue	80p	—
			ii) Will's Specialities Issue	40p	—
		52	Birds of Brilliant Plumage:—		
			A. Four Aces Issue (1924)	£1.00	—
			B. Pirate Issue:—		
			i) With border on front (1914)	80p	—
			ii) Without border on front (1916)	80p	—
			C. Red Star, Circle and Leaves Issue	£1.50	—
		25	Birds of the East 1st Series Ruby Queen Issue	50p	£12.50
		25	Birds of the East 2nd Series Ruby Queen Issue	50p	£12.50
127		36	Boxers (1911–12)		
			A. Scissors Issue	£1.50	£54.00
			B. Green Star and Circle Issue	£2.00	£72.00
62			Britains Defenders (1915–16):—		
			A. Will's Specialities Issue:—		
		50	i) Inscribed "S Series of 50"	80p	£40.00
		8	ii) Without Inscription "A Series of 50"	£4.00	—
		50	B. Havelock Issue	£1.75	—
		50	C. Scissors Issue:—		
			i) Red Upright "Scissors" Packet	50p	£25.00
			ii) Green Upright "Scissors" Packet	50p	£25.00
			iii) Red Slanting "Scissors" Packet	40p	£20.00
		50	D. Green Star and Circle Issue	80p	—
		43	British Army Boxers (1913–14) Scissors Issue	80p	£35.00
137		50	British Army Uniforms (1905–10):—		
			A. Wild Woodbine Issue	£1.50	£75.00
			B. Flag Issue	£1.50	—
			C. Scissors Issue	£1.50	£75.00
		100	British Beauties (1910–18)	60p	—
		50	British Empire Series (1913):—		
			A. Capstan Issue	40p	£20.00
			B. Havelock Issue	90p	—
			C. Vice Regal Issue	40p	£20.00
	P	48	British Royal and Ancient Buildings (1925–30)	20p	£10.00
		45	British Rugby Players (1930)	80p	—
		50	Chateaux (1925–30)	£1.50	£75.00
134		50	Children of All Nations (1925–30)	30p	£15.00
133		100	China's Famous Warriors (1911) Pirate Issue Ref. 357 (1911):—		
			A. First 25 Subjects	25p	£12.50
			B. Second 25 Subjects	25p	£12.50
			C. Third 25 Subjects	25p	£12.50
			D. Fourth 25 Subjects	25p	£12.50
		28	Chinese Actors and Actresses (1907) Pirate Issue Ref. 361	80p	—
		25	Chinese Beauties 1st Series Pirate Issue Ref. 362 (1907):—		
			A. Vertical Back	60p	£15.00
			B. Horizontal Back	80p	£20.00
		25	Chinese Beauties 2nd Series Pirate Issue Ref. 363 (1909):—		

Illus. No.	Size	Number in set		Price per card	Complete set
			A. With Framelines on Front	60p	£15.00
			B. Without Framelines on Front	60p	£15.00
		30	Chinese Children's Games (1905–15) Ruby Queen Issue Ref. 364	80p	—
		50	Chinese Costumes Pirate Issue (1928) Ref. 365	£1.50	—
	EL	25	Chinese Pagodas (1905–10) Pirate Issue Ref. 366	—	—
		50	Chinese Proverbs Brown Ref. 367 (1928):—		
			A. Pirate Issue	60p	—
			B. Ruby Queen Issue	£1.50	—
		50	Chinese Proverbs Coloured (1914–16) Pirate Issue Ref. 368:—		
			A. Back in Blue:—		
			i) Without Overprint	80p	—
			ii) With Overprint	90p	—
			B. Back in Olive Green	£1.00	—
		40	Chinese Trades (1900–05) Autocar Issue	—	—
		50	Chinese Transport (1914) Ref. 370 Ruby Queen Issue	80p	—
		50	Cinema Stars Four Aces Issue (1922–30):—		
			A. Numbered	75p	£37.50
			B. Unnumbered	50p	£25.00
		25	Cinema Stars (1922–30) Scissors Issue	70p	£17.50
64		50	Coaches and Coaching Days (1925–30)	50p	£25.00
			Conundrums:—		
		25	A. With Album Clause	£4.00	—
		25	B. Without Album Clause	£4.00	—
		25	C. Without Album Clause Redrawn	£4.00	—
		50	D. Without Album Clause Inscribed "50 Different …"	£4.00	—
	M	68	Crests & Colours of Australian Universities, Colleges & Schools (1922)	25p	£17.00
	P	63	Cricketers Ref. 59E	£3.00	—
		25	Cricketer Series Ref. 59F	£30.00	—
		50	Cricketer Series (1901–02) Ref. 59G	£30.00	—
129	P	48	Cricket Season (1928–29)	£1.00	—
135		27	Dancing Girls (1915) Scissors Issue:—		
			A. Inscribed "28 Subjects" (No. 3 not issued)	£1.00	£27.00
			B. Inscribed "27 Subjects"	£1.00	£27.00
		25	Derby Day Series (1910–25):—		
			A. Scissors Issue:—		
			i) With Title	80p	£20.00
			ii) Without Title	£3.00	—
			B. Star & Circle Issue	£2.00	—
71		50	Dogs – Scenic Backgrounds (1925–26)	15p	£7.50
	M	20	Dogs – Heads 1st Series (1927–28):—		
			A. Will's World Renown Cigarettes Issue:—		
			i) With Album Clause	80p	—
			ii) Without Album Clause	80p	—
			B. Three Castles and Vice Regal Cigarettes Issue	80p	—
	M	20	Dogs-Heads 2nd Series (1927–28)	50p	—
136		32	Drum Horses (1905–10):—		
			A. Scissors Issue:—		
			i) Vertical Format, Open Scissors Packet	£2.00	—
			ii) Horizontal Format, Closed Scissors Packet	£2.00	£65.00
			B. United Service Issue	£2.50	—
			C. Green Star Circle & Leaves Issue	£2.00	—
	P	25	English Cricketers (1926)	80p	£20.00
	M	25	English Period Costumes (1928):—		
			A. White Card	80p	—
			B. Cream Card	50p	£12.50
			Etchings (of Dogs):—		
		26	A. Small Size English Language Issues:—		
			i) With "Gold Flake Cigarettes"	£2.00	—
			ii) Without Gold Flake Cigarettes (1925)	30p	£7.50
		26	B. Small Size Dutch Language Issues:—		
			i) With Framelines to back	£3.00	—
			ii) Without Framelines to back	£3.00	—
	M	26	C. Medium Size (1925)	40p	£10.00
		25	The Evolution of the British Navy (1910–15)	80p	£20.00
			Famous Film Stars (1934):—		
		100	A. Small Size	25p	—
	M	100	B. Medium Size:—		
			i) White Card	25p	—
			ii) Cream Card	25p	—
	MP	100	Famous Film Stars (1925–30)	80p	—
		50	Famous Footballers (1914–15):—		
			A. Scissors Issue	80p	£40.00
			B. Star & Circle Issue	£1.25	—
		50	Famous Inventions (Without I.T.C. Clause) (1927)	30p	£15.00
		75	Film Favourites Four Aces Issue (1925–30)	50p	£37.50
		50	Fish of Australasia (1912):—		
			A. Capstan Issue	50p	£25.00
			B. Havelock Issue	£1.00	—
			C. Vice Regal Issue	50p	£25.00
			Flag Girls of All Nations:—		
		50	A. Capstan Issue	80p	—
		50	B. Vice-Regal Issue	80p	—
		25	C. United Service Issue	£1.00	£25.00
		25	D. Scissors Issue:—		
			i) Numbered	£1.25	—
			ii) Unnumbered	£2.00	—

Illus. No.	Size	Number in set		Price per card	Complete set
55		25	E. Green Star Circle & Leaves Issue	80p	£20.00
		8	Flags Shaped Metal (1915)	£4.00	—
58		126	Flags & Ensigns (1903–10)	50p	£63.00
		25	Flags of the Empire (No I.T.C. Clause)	—	—
			Flowers Purple Mountain Issue:—		
		20	A. Numbered..................................	£3.00	—
		100	B. Unnumbered................................	£4.00	—
56		50	Football Club Colours Scissors/Special Army Quality Issue (1905–10)	£1.00	
		28	Football Club Colours and Flags (1905–15):—		
			A. Capstan Issue..............................	£1.50	£42.00
			B. Havelock Issue	£4.00	
		200	Footballers (1933):—		
			A. Small Size	40p	—
			B. Medium Size	80p	—
		50	Girls of All Nations (1905–10):—		
			A. Capstan Issue..............................	80p	—
			B. Vice Regal Issue	80p	—
			C. Green Star Circle and Leaves Issue...........	80p	—
		25	Governors – General of India Scissors Issue (1911)	£2.50	£62.50
	M	25	Heraldic Signs and Their Origins (1925)..................	50p	£12.50
		30	Heroic Deeds (1914) Scissors Issue.....................	£1.00	£30.00
188		50	Historic Events (1912):—		
			A. Will's Specialities Issue.....................	40p	£20.00
			B. Havelock Issue	£1.50	—
	M	25	History of Naval Dress (1930)...........................	—	—
	P	50	Homeland Events (1925–30)	20p	£10.00
		50	Horses of Today (1906):—		
			A. Capstan Issue..............................	60p	—
			B. Havelock Issue	£2.00	—
			C. Vice Regal Issue	60p	—
		50	Household Hints (1927–30):—		
			A. With "Will's Cigarettes" at Top Back	40p	—
			B. Without Will's Cigarettes at Top Back	60p	—
			Houses of Parliament (1905–10):—		
60		33	A. Pirate Issue................................	50p	£17.00
		32	B. Star and Circle Issue	60p	£20.00
		50	Indian Regiments (1905–10):—		
			A. Scissors Issue..............................	£2.00	—
			B. Star and Circle Issue	£2.25	—
		50	Interesting Buildings (1905)	80p	£40.00
		67	International Footballers Season 1909–1910:—		
			A. Scissors Issue (1910)	£2.00	—
			B. United Services Issue (1910)	£2.00	—
			C. Flag Issue (1911)...........................	£2.00	—
54		50	Jiu-Jitsu (1905–10):—		
			A. Scissors Issue..............................	£1.50	£75.00
			B. Flag Issue	£1.50	—
		53	Jockeys and Owners Colours with P.C. Inset Scissors Issue (1905–10)	£2.50	—
53		50	Lighthouses (1925–30)	25p	£12.50
		45	Melbourne Cup Winners (1906)	£1.50	—
61		50	Merchant Ships of the World (1925–30) (Without I.T.C. Clause)	30p	£15.00
		40	Merrie England Studies (Male) (1905–15)	£2.00	—
		24	Merveilles du Monde (1927)..............................	£2.00	—
		25	Military Portraits (1917) Scissors Issue..................	£2.00	—
	M	25	Miniatures – Oval Medallions (1914)	£30.00	—
	K	25	Miniature Playing Cards Scissors Issue	£3.00	—
		50	Modern War Weapons (1916):—		
			A. Wills Specialities Issue	60p	—
			B. Havelock Issue	£2.00	—
		25	Modes of Conveyance (1925–30) Four Aces Issue	80p	£20.00
		48	Motor Cars (1924).....................................	60p	£30.00
74	P	50	Motor Cars (1928).....................................	40p	£20.00
72		50	Motor Cycles (1926)	70p	£35.00
	P	48	Movie Stars (1925–30)	£2.00	—
		50	Music Hall Celebrities (1906–11) Scissors Issue..........	£1.50	£75.00
		50	National Flags and Arms (1930–35)	60p	—
	M	25	The Nation's Shrines (1925–30).........................	50p	£12.50
	P	50	Nature Studies (1925–30)	70p	—
		50	New Zealand Birds (1925–30)	35p	£17.50
73	P	50	New Zealand – Early Scenes & Maori Life (1925–30)	20p	£10.00
		50	New Zealand Footballers (1928).........................	25p	£12.50
		50	New Zealand Race Horses (1928):—		
			A. Cream Card	30p	£15.00
			B. White Card................................	50p	
198		50	N.Z. Butterflies, Moths & Beetles (1925–30)................	30p	£15.00
205		25	Past and Present (1929)	50p	£12.50
		50	Past and Present Champions (1905–10):—		
			A. Capstan Cigarette Issue	£3.00	—
			B. Capstan Tobacco Issue......................	£5.00	—
204		25	Picturesque People of the Empire (1925–30)...............	50p	£12.50
63		25	Pirates and Highwaymen (1925–30)......................	50p	£12.50
128		25	Police of the World (1905–10)	£3.00	£75.00
	M	70	Practical Wireless (1922–30)............................	80p	—
		50	Products of the World – Maps and Scenes (1905–10):—		
			A. Pirate Issue................................	60p	—
			B. Green Star Circle and Leaves Issue	£1.00	—

Illus. No.	Size	Number in set		Price per card	Complete set
		50	Products of the World – Scenes only (1929).................	25p	£12.50
		50	Prominent Australian and English Cricketers (1907) Ref. 59H	£3.50	—
		23	Prominent Australian and English Cricketers (1907–08) Ref. 59I	£4.00	—
131		59	Prominent Australian and English Cricketers (1911) Ref. 59J:—		
			A. Capstan Issue:—		
			i) "A Series of 50"	£3.50	—
			ii) "A Series of .../A Series of 59"	£3.50	—
			B. Vice Regal Issue:—		
			i) "A Series of 50"	£3.50	—
			ii) "A Series of .../A Series of 59"	£3.50	—
			C. Havelock Issue	£10.00	—
		25	Puzzle Series (1910–15) Scissors/United Service Issue	£2.00	—
		50	Races of Mankind (1905–10)	£3.00	—
59		50	Railway Engines (1924)	40p	£20.00
		50	Railway Working (1925–30).....................	80p	£40.00
65		50	Regimental colours and Cap Badges (1910–15):—		
			A. Scissors Issue	60p	£30.00
			B. United Service Issue:—		
			i) Red Back......................	40p	£20.00
			ii) Blue Back	40p	£20.00
		33	Regimental Pets (1905–10) Scissors Issue..................	£2.00	—
57		50	Regimental Standards and Cap Badges (1930)...............	30p	£15.00
		50	Riders of the World:—		
			A. Capstan/Vice Regal/Pennant/Will's Specialities Issue (1913)......................	80p	—
			B. Havelock Issue (1913).....................	£2.00	—
			C. Back in Red-Brown (1925–30).............	50p	£25.00
		50	Romance of the Heavens (1928) (No I.T.C. Clause)...........	60p	
130		25	Roses (1912):—		
			A. Purple Mountain Issues:—		
			i) With Will's Cigarettes on Front	£2.50	—
			ii) Without Will's Cigarettes on Front	£2.00	—
			B. Plain Backs with Will's Cigarettes on Front	—	—
	P	50	The Royal Family at Home and Abroad (1930–35)	50p	
		50	Royal Mail (With Will's Cigarettes on Fronts):—		
			A. Capstan Issue.....................	70p	£35.00
			B. Havelock Issue	£2.00	—
			C. Vice Regal Issue	70p	£35.00
			D. With Anonymous Backs	£3.00	—
			E. With Plain Back	£3.00	—
	P	50	The Royal Navy (1925–30).....................	50p	£25.00
		100	Royalty, Notabilities and Events in Russia, China and South Africa (1900–02)	70p	£70.00
		27	Rulers of the World (1911)	£3.00	—
			Russo-Japanese Series (1905–06):—		
		100	A. Fronts in Black	60p	£60.00
		50	B. Fronts in Red	£3.00	—
126		50	Safety First (1934–35).....................	50p	£25.00
	LP	48	Scenes from the Empire (1930–35)	50p	£25.00
		30	Semaphore Signalling (1910–15)	£1.00	£30.00
66	P	50	Ships and Shipping (1928).....................	20p	£10.00
		36	Ships and Their Pennants (1910–15)	£1.50	—
		50	Ships' Badges (1926).....................	50p	£25.00
79		50	Signalling Series (1913):—		
			A. Capstan Issue.....................	40p	£20.00
			B. Havelock Issue	60p	—
			C. Vice Regal Issue	40p	£20.00
		40	Sketches in Black and White (1900–05)	£1.00	—
			Soldiers of the World:—		
		50	A. Numbered.....................	£3.00	—
		75	B. Unnumbered	£3.50	—
		99	South African Personalities (1900).....................	—	—
		30	Sporting Girls (1900–10) Scissors Issue.....................	£1.50	—
75	P	50	A Sporting Holiday in New Zealand (1925–30):—		
			A. Small Size	20p	£10.00
			B. Medium Size	30p	£15.00
		25	Sporting Terms (1905–10):—		
			A. Capstan Issue.....................	£2.50	—
			B. Vice Regal Issue	£2.50	—
		50	Sports of the World (1917)	£1.00	—
		50	Stage & Music Hall Celebrities (1900–05) (Portrait in Oval Frame):—		
			A. Capstan Issue.....................	£1.00	—
			B. Vice Regal Issue	£1.00	—
			C. Havelock Issue	£1.00	£50.00
		50	Stage and Music Hall Celebrities (1900–05) (Portrait in Oblong Frame)	£1.25	£62.50
	P	52	Stars of the Cinema (1925–26):—		
			A. Text Back	£1.50	—
			B. Four Aces Issue	£1.00	—
67		50	Time & Money in Different Countries (1908):—		
			A. Capstan Issue.....................	40p	—
			B. Havelock Issue	£1.50	—
			C. Vice Regal Issue:—		
			i) With album Clause	40p	£20.00
			ii) Without album clause.....................	40p	£20.00

W. D. & H. O. WILLS (continued)

Illus. No.	Size	Number in set		Price per card	Complete set
		50	A Tour Round the World (1907)	80p	—
		50	Types of the British Army (1905–10):—		
			A. Capstan Issue..	£1.25	—
			B. Vice Regal Issue	£1.25	—
		50	Types of the Commonwealth Military Forces (1910–15):—		
			A. Capstan Issue..	£1.50	—
			B. Vice Regal Issue	£1.50	—
			C. Havelock Issue	£1.75	—
		25	United States Warships (1911):—		
			A. Capstan Issue..	£1.00	—
			B. Havelock Issue	£1.50	—
			C. Vice Regal Issue	£1.00	—
77	P	50	Units of the British Army and RAF (1925–30).............	20p	£10.00
		50	U.S.S. Co's Steamers (1930)...............................	70p	—
		50	V.C.'s (1925–30)..	50p	£25.00
68		25	Victoria Cross Heroes:—		
			A. Havelock Issue	£1.50	£37.50
			B. Will's Specialities Issue.............................	80p	£20.00
			C. Scissors Issue	80p	£20.00
		10	Victorian Football Association (1905–10):—		
			A. Capstan on Front.....................................	£3.00	—
			B. Havelock on Front....................................	—	—
		19	Victorian Football League (1905–10):—		
			A. Capstan on Front.....................................	£3.00	—
			B. Havelock on Front....................................	£4.00	—
		215	Views of the World (1905–10):—		
			A. Numbers 1–50 Plain Backs (Anonymous)	30p	
			B. Numbers 51–215 Blue Back Capstan Issue	30p	
			C. Numbers 51–215 Green Back Vice Regal Issue	30p	
		25	Village Models Series (1925–30):—		
			A. Small Size	80p	£20.00
			B. Medium Size	£1.00	—
76		50	War Incidents 1st Series (1916):—		
			A. Will's Specialities Issue.............................	60p	—
			B. Havelock Issue	£1.50	—
			C. Scissors Issue	50p	£25.00
		50	War Incidents 2nd Series (1917):—		
			A. Will's Specialities Issue.............................	60p	£30.00
			B. Havelock Issue	£4.00	—
		50	War Pictures (1915):—		
			A. Will's Specialities Issue.............................	50p	£25.00
			B. Havelock Issue	£1.00	—
		50	Warships (1925)	50p	£25.00
		30	What It Means (1910–17) Scissors Issue...................	50p	£15.00
			Wild Animals:—		
70		50	A. Small Size titled "Wild Animals" Heads...............	20p	£10.00
	M	25	B. Medium Size titled "Wild Animals"..................	40p	£10.00
		50	Wild Animals of the World:—		
			A. Bristol & London Issue..............................	£3.00	—
			B. Celebrated Cigarettes Issue..........................	£1.25	£62.50
			C. Star, Circle & Leaves Issue	£1.50	—
69		25	Wonders of the World (1925–30)	40p	£10.00
80		25	The World's Dreadnoughts (1910):—		
			A. Capstan Issue..	60p	—
			B. Vice Regal Issue	60p	—
			C. No I.T.C. Clauses....................................	50p	£12.50
78		50	Zoo (1925–30):—		
			A. Scissors Issue without descriptive back	—	—
			B. Will's Issue with descriptive back	20p	£10.00
		50	Zoological Series (1922–30)	80p	—

C. Silk Issues 1911–17

	Size	Number in set		Price per card	Complete set
	M	50	Arms of the British Empire..............................	£1.00	—
	M	50	Australian Butterflies...................................	£1.00	—
	M	50	Birds & Animals of Australia.............................	£1.00	—
	M	50	Crests & Colours of Australian Universities, Colleges & Schools...	£1.00	—
	EL	1	Flag	—	—
		28	Flags of 1914–18 Allies:—		
			A. Backs with letterpress in Capitals	£1.00	—
			B. Backs with letterpress in small lettering	£1.00	—
		38	Kings & Queens of England	£2.00	—
	M	50	Popular Flowers:—		
			A. Backs Inscribed "Now being inserted in the large packets"...	£2.00	—
			B. Backs Inscribed "Now being inserted in the 1/- packets"	£2.00	—
	M	67	War Medals...	£1.50	—

J. WIX & SONS LTD.

	Size	Number in set		Price per card	Complete set
	P	24	Royal Tour of New Zealand (1925–30).....................	£3.00	—

GEO. F. YOUNG & BRO., U.S.A.

	Size	Number in set		Price per card	Complete set
	L	?	Actresses (1885–95).....................................	£6.00	—